Since Vietnam

The United States in World Affairs, 1973–1995

America in Crisis

A series of books on American Diplomatic History

Since Vietnam

The United States in World Affairs, 1973–1995

H. W. Brands

Professor of History
Texas A & M University

McGraw-Hill, Inc.

New York   St. Louis   San Francisco   Auckland   Bogotá   Caracas   Lisbon
London   Madrid   Mexico City   Milan   Montreal   New Delhi   San Juan
Singapore   Sydney   Tokyo   Toronto

This book was set in Palatino by Graphic World, Inc.
The editors were Peter Labella and Caroline Iannuzzo;
the production supervisor was Friederich W. Schulte.
The cover was designed by Carol A. Couch.
New maps were rendered by Mapping Specialists Limited.
R. R. Donnelley & Sons Company was printer and binder.

SINCE VIETNAM
The United States in World Affairs, 1973–1995

This book is printed on recycled, acid-free paper containing
10% postconsumer waste.

2 3 4 5 6 7 8 9 0 DOC DOC 9 0 9 8 7 6

ISBN 0-07-007196-9

Library of Congress Cataloging-in-Publication Data

Brands, H. W.
    Since Vietnam: the United States in world affairs, 1973–1995 /
  H. W. Brands.
        p.   cm.
    Includes bibliographical references and index.
    ISBN 0-07-007196-9
    1. United States—Foreign relations—1945–1989.   2. United States—
Foreign relations—1989-   I. Title.
E840.B73   1996
327.73—dc20   95-2756

About the Author

H. W. Brands grew up in Oregon before earning history degrees from Stanford University and the University of Texas at Austin. He has taught at the University of Texas and Vanderbilt University, in addition to Texas A & M University, where he is currently professor of history. This is his tenth book on American history and international relations.

Contents

Preface

It is now nearly a quarter century since the last American soldiers left Vietnam. During that time the landscape of international affairs has changed almost beyond recognition. Occasional landmarks retain their old significance, but others have been utterly transformed, and many have vanished altogether. Washington is still the capital of the planet's most powerful country, although the "Free World" that it was also the capital of is rarely mentioned anymore. Moscow, once the command post of an enormous Eurasian empire, is now merely a run-down city of 10 million survivors of a discredited ideology. The Berlin Wall, long the symbol of the struggle between Washington and Moscow, has been jackhammered to bits, parceled into as many pieces as the True Cross and offered for sale in gift shops around the globe.

The Vietnam War traumatized the American political system, and the effects of that trauma have played themselves out in American foreign policy ever since. One conclusion many Americans drew from the defeat in Vietnam was that the principles that had guided American policy since the beginning of the Cold War were obsolete. The principles may have fit the world of the late 1940s (some really disillusioned types said they had been wrong even then), but by the early 1970s that world had disappeared. Military force was giving way to economic prowess, whether measured by robotic manufacturing techniques or millions of barrels of petroleum production per day. Conflicts in Africa and Latin America spilled beyond those areas and chronically entangled the superpowers. Scores of governments that hadn't existed a generation earlier clamored to be heard, and often succeeded. The two great alliance systems that had arisen from the wreckage of World War II had grown outmoded as the threats against which they had been designed were supplanted by threats the designers hadn't foreseen. In the case of the Soviet alliance system, it had been shattered by the defection of China, which now hurled invectives and worse at its erstwhile sponsor.

A second reaction to Vietnam required longer to gain a grip on the American psyche. This held that the world really hadn't changed, at least not in essentials. The failure in Vietnam wasn't a matter of principles mistaken but of principles misapplied. The existential global struggle remained as before: America versus the Soviet Union, democracy versus communism, good versus evil. Such new phenomena as were arising were merely ephemera; the values that had guided American policy since 1945 were as vital as ever.

In its dazed post-Vietnam condition, the American political system lurched between these two contradictory worldviews. Jimmy Carter, the first president elected after the fall of Saigon, initially subscribed to the new-world interpretation. Carter contended that human rights abuse and global poverty, not communism, were the primary threats to planetary peace and American security. For too long had American policy been merely reactive; for too long had Americans allowed others to set their priorities. The new world was one in which Americans must live up to their ideals, not down to their fears.

When Carter's born-again idealism failed to deliver the millennium in the requisite quadrennium, Americans turned to an expositor of the opposite gospel. Ronald Reagan proclaimed that nothing important had changed since 1945—or perhaps 1917. The communists might have shifted tactics, but their strategy of world conquest remained as before. And so, consequently, must the American strategy of resisting communism at every turn. Military might was the language Moscow understood; in military might America must speak. Compromise was appeasement; appeasement was simply disaster deferred.

Reality took about as long to blast Reagan's nothing-has-changed interpretation of international affairs as it had to explode Carter's everything-has-changed view. The fact of the matter was that much had changed but much remained the same. The superpower duopoly of the early Cold War had indeed been broken by new claimants to power, of whom several based their claims on economic instruments rather than the traditional military devices. And the peace of the planet was almost certainly at smaller risk from a hypothetical Third World War than from the actual and multiple Third World wars. But the fundamental nature of international affairs hadn't changed. States were still the operative units, and they still vied for power. The strong did what they wanted, the weak what the strong allowed.

The story of American foreign relations since Vietnam is the story of how Americans came to terms—and, more frequently, failed to come to terms—with the muddy complexity of life in the late twentieth century. The aftereffects of Vietnam were one cause of the failures; American history and American politics were two others. For most of their national existence, Americans had held aloof from world affairs, engaging only in those that suited their taste and then largely on their own terms. Pearl Harbor assassinated American aloofness, but the war that followed presented the world in terms as Manichean and stark as they ever get here below, and it was easy for Americans to project those terms forward onto the postwar period. Though Vietnam sorely tested—refuted, for those with open minds —that projection, it didn't at all diminish Americans' desire for the simplicity the projection embodied. If anything, it intensified the desire.

So did the American political system. American politics is the art of reductionism. In the voting booth, voters choose this candidate or that; almost never do they get a genuine third choice. Such a situation encourages, if not forces, candidates to paint themselves and their opponents in black-and-white, either-or terms. Either the status quo is horrible and everything needs to be changed, which is to say, "Throw the rascals out;" or the status quo is basically sound and the incumbents should be kept. The problem of reductionism is especially marked in matters of foreign policy, since most voters attend to foreign policy only when shouted at. Now and then the world does the shouting; frequently it's done by politicians. Neither lends itself to nuance or subtlety.

Between the politics of reductionism and the yearning for simplicity, Americans after Vietnam had great difficulty accepting the complexity of the world they lived in. Sometimes they overcame the difficulty; sometimes the difficulty overcame them. What follows is the tale of both outcomes.

I would like to thank Robert Divine for his usual cogent comments on an early version of this book. The thorough reading and pertinent suggestions provided by David Colburn, University of Florida; Nicholas Cullather, Indiana University; Herbert Druks, CUNY Brooklyn College; James Giglio, Southwest Missouri State University; Ann Heiss, Kent State University; John Jameson, Kent State University; Clayton Koppes, Oberlin College; and Steven Lawson,

University of North Carolina, have also been valuable, even where the suggestions have contradicted one another. Peter Labella, Caroline Iannuzzo, and the others at McGraw-Hill are still their professional selves.

H. W. Brands

Since Vietnam
The United States in World Affairs, 1973–1995

CHAPTER 1

The Old Order Totters: 1973–1977

As long as the fate of Vietnam hung in the balance, the full trauma of America's defeat there remained in the future, and Americans were able to assess the world in comparatively objective terms. Few denied that a great deal had changed in international affairs since the beginning of the Cold War. The centerpiece of American Cold War policy, the containment of communism, had collided head-on with the intransigent nationalism of Ho Chi Minh and his Vietnamese followers and had been severely damaged in the collision. By January 1973, when Washington and Hanoi signed the Paris agreement that called for the withdrawal of the last American troops from Vietnam, containment appeared all but defunct—and not simply because of the situation in Vietnam. Other actions taken somewhat more freely by the Nixon administration were even more damaging to containment. In 1971 Richard Nixon had astounded the world by announcing that he would travel to China to begin normalizing relations with the Asian communist giant. By this single stroke Nixon undercut the basic objective of American postwar policy in Asia: to corral China. Simultaneously with his opening to Beijing, Nixon moved toward better relations with the Soviet Union, the original and primary target of containment. Detente, as the new policy was called, transformed Moscow from mortal enemy to amicable, or at least cordial, competitor. Considered together, the American withdrawal from Vietnam, the opening to China, and detente with the Soviet Union essentially eviscerated containment.

But the gutting of containment told only half the story of the 1970s. The collapse of the postwar international economic structure was at least equally important. From World War II until the late 1960s, the United States had been the locomotive of international economic development. Under a financial regime established at the 1944 Bretton Woods economic conference, the American economy

1

produced unprecedented prosperity for the American people and unmatched trade opportunities for America's economic partners, several of whom converted those opportunities into unexampled prosperity for their own peoples. Throughout this period of American dominance, the American dollar was the defining standard of the world's currencies. But by the early 1970s, a combination of economic growth among America's trade partners and inflationary policies in the United States had eroded the hegemony of the dollar, forcing a historic readjustment of the world's major currencies.

Adding to the strains on the Bretton Woods system was the overnight shift of wealth from oil-consuming countries to oil producers. Until the early 1970s, world petroleum-production capacity had outstripped demand sufficiently that prices remained relatively low. During the early 1970s, however, demand caught up with supply, allowing producers to raise prices by capping output. The producers capped with a vengeance, quadrupling oil prices in the space of a few months and turning the international economy on its ear. Oil ministers from countries 95 percent of the world's population had never heard of before—countries such as Kuwait, Gabon, and Qatar—now held the fate of some of the planet's most powerful nations in their hands. While American motorists fumed at the prices they were paying for gasoline, American homeowners stared in disbelief at their heating bills, and American workers in energy-intensive industries wondered how long they would keep their jobs.

Between the political transformations caused by the eclipse of containment and the economic upheavals occasioned by the oil-price revolution and the collapse of the Bretton Woods system, the American government and the American people spent the mid-1970s reevaluating their country's approach to world affairs. That the reevaluation took place during and just after the final act of the Vietnam War made it only more difficult.

1. THE SHADOW OF VIETNAM

Richard Nixon subsequently liked to claim that the withdrawal of the last American troops from Vietnam in March 1973 represented not a failure of American policy but rather its success. Few people believed him, at least at first; after Watergate the former president had a rather serious credibility problem. But he hammered away nonetheless, explaining that the American withdrawal was the logical culmination of the policy of "Vietnamization," which substituted South Vietnamese soldiers for Americans in the defense of South Vietnam, but which also called for continuing American military and economic aid to Saigon and the application of American air power against the North Vietnamese.

Nixon's protestations notwithstanding, most observers interpreted the American withdrawal as an admission that South Vietnam couldn't be defended at acceptable cost to the United States. Few could figure out how South Vietnam would be able to defend itself without American troops when it hadn't been able to defend itself with the help of half a million Americans. Even more to the point, whatever the military significance of the American withdrawal, that withdrawal represented the undeniable political fact that the American people were losing interest in Vietnam. Nixon might promise aid and air support to Saigon, but Congress showed no enthusiasm for investing more money and possibly more lives in South Vietnam. That by early 1973 the murky waters of Watergate were rising around the president's ankles only hastened what would have happened anyway: during the summer of 1973 Congress mandated an end to American bombing missions in Indochina. And the legislature consistently authorized less aid than the Nixon administration claimed was necessary for the defense of South Vietnam.

Given this situation, to most onlookers it appeared only a matter of time before the peace accord of January 1973 would break down. Hardly anyone believed that the Vietnamese communists had spent a generation fighting to reunify their country only to abandon their quest on the verge of victory. As events proved, they hadn't, and after waiting for the United States to lose the last of its desire to defend South Vietnam they mounted their final offensive. This campaign, which commenced in the first part of 1975, succeeded with a swiftness that surprised even the communists. By the early spring, South Vietnamese forces were on the run everywhere. The end came in April when the communists captured Saigon.

The frantic and tragic scenes that surrounded the fall of Saigon drove home the depth of the debacle into which Nixon and his predecessors had driven the United States. America's Vietnamese allies scrambled, pushed, clawed, and bribed their way onto the last trucks, planes, and helicopters leaving the capital. Knowing that their lives were forfeit on account of their recent connections, some of those who couldn't find places inside took the desperate measure of clinging to the skids of the helicopters lifting off of the roof of the American embassy.

The memories of those scenes joined other images seared into the American psyche by the most divisive war in the nation's modern history: appalling pictures of naked children running screaming from American napalm attacks; of Saigon's intelligence chief personally blowing out the brains of a suspected Vietcong guerrilla; of monks staring serenely through the flames that were consuming their flesh, flames they themselves had lit in protest against the government the United States was supporting. The war had corrupted the language and those who spoke it: villages were destroyed in order to be "saved"; "body counts" lumped friends with enemies to mask the failure of American policy.

The images of Vietnam and the powerful feelings they evoked colored American attitudes and policies for the next twenty years. Starting while the fighting was still going, Americans of all political persuasions argued over why the American side was losing the war. Left-leaners (whose numbers were tremendously swelled by the war) saw the failure in Vietnam as implicit in the policy of containment. America had never possessed the power to garrison the entire world against communism, these critics said. (The real radicals said the United States had no right even to try.) American policy was like a drunk driver—drunk on illusions of omnipotence, in this case; if the wreck hadn't occurred in Vietnam it would have happened somewhere else. Moderate critics of the war blamed the particular circumstances of Vietnam. Had the South Vietnamese been able to create a stable government—the way the South Koreans had, for example—they would have been able to beat back the challenge from the Vietcong and the North Vietnamese. Conservatives joined Richard Nixon in laying the blame on the steps of the American Capitol, charging Congress with betraying Saigon at the moment of victory. "The war and peace in Indochina that America had won at such cost over twelve years of sacrifice and fighting were lost within a matter of months once Congress refused to fulfill our obligations," Nixon wrote. Defenders of the military complained that American soldiers had been forced to fight with one hand tied behind their backs. If the politicians in Washington had

had the nerve to go all out for victory, the American military would have brought it home.[1]

For all the debate, everyone agreed on one thing: that Vietnam shouldn't be repeated. The slogan "No more Vietnams" carried different implications for different people, but its basic thrust was plain enough. A relative few advocated a retreat to a kind of neo-isolationism, with Americans looking after their own and leaving the rest of the world to fend for itself. A larger number counseled concentration on the overseas commitments that were central to American security: the NATO alliance, the treaty with Japan, the defense of the Western Hemisphere. Many suggested that the United States should spend its resources and energy on improving America's economic competitiveness at a time when American industrial supremacy could no longer be taken for granted.

The backlash from Vietnam assumed more-specific shapes as well. In November 1973, Congress passed the War Powers Act, which required any president to consult with the legislature before committing American troops to combat and mandated that the president bring those troops home within ninety days unless Congress explicitly granted an extension. Since the beginning of the Cold War, Congress had acquiesced in increasing presidential control of foreign policy, especially military policy, to the point of allowing the White House to wage two full-blown wars, in Korea and Vietnam, without bothering to request a congressional declaration of war. The War Powers Act represented a belated effort on the part of the legislative branch to reclaim some of its authority from the executive branch.

The War Powers Act also signaled a belief on the part of legislators that presidents couldn't be trusted. The term "credibility gap" had first arisen in the context of the 1965 American intervention in the Dominican Republic, when Lyndon Johnson justified his action on grounds that communists were about to take over that country. Johnson absurdly exaggerated the danger, as reporters soon discovered; the rift between White House release and Dominican reality became the original credibility gap. The gap yawned wider when the Tet offensive of 1968 exploded Johnson's predictions that victory in Vietnam was nigh. Richard Nixon extended the excavation

[1]Richard Nixon, *The Memoirs of Richard Nixon* (New York, 1978), 889.

with his 1968 promise of a "secret plan" to end the war: the secret was that the war would spread, spilling into Laos and Cambodia. (Henry Kissinger explained the discrepancy between promise and fulfillment: "The pledges of each new Administration," he said, "are like leaves on a turbulent sea.") Nixon's credibility gap eventually included Watergate, which destroyed his presidency and set public trust in elected officials back a generation—and counting, as of the mid-1990s.[2]

Popular distrust of Washington only increased as congressional investigations into the Watergate affair revealed a long history of unsavory activities by the American government in pursuit of its Cold War objectives against the communists. Americans were dismayed to learn that agents of their government had assisted in the overthrow of the elected governments of Iran and Guatemala during the 1950s; had conspired to assassinate Fidel Castro of Cuba and Patrice Lumumba of the Congo (Zaire) during the 1960s; had doped unwitting subjects, including U.S. citizens, with mind-altering drugs (apparently driving at least one man to suicide); and had illegally opened mail and conducted intelligence operations within the United States. Once the congressional inquiry began revealing the government's soiled laundry, disillusioned former insiders added to the pile with memoirs and exposés of their own. Nor had the dirty tricks ended long ago: as recently as 1973, American agents had helped destabilize the Chilean government of Marxist Salvador Allende, contributing to Allende's downfall and violent death (whether by murder or suicide hadn't been proven and still wouldn't be, as of the mid-1990s) and his replacement by the ferociously right-wing General Augusto Pinochet.

These revelations intensified the backlash against the Cold War policies that had led the United States into Vietnam. From all across the political spectrum demands arose that the secret warriors be brought to heel. "The problem that confronts us," the liberal *Progressive* declared, "is not just that the C.I.A. occasionally lapses into illegal activities, but that it is, inherently, an illegitimate enterprise." A writer in *The Nation* asserted, "The Central Intelligence Agency was founded on cold-war premises, assigned to beat the bad guys by hook or crook, advised that the phrase 'national security' would be employed on the highest levels to justify any damn thing that

[2]Seymour M. Hersh, *The Price of Power* (New York, 1983), 28.

went right or wrong." Centrist *Newsweek* carried an article entitled bluntly, "Abolish the C.I.A.!" The author explained that the intelligence activities of the C.I.A. could be shifted to the State Department and other agencies, while the "dirty tricks" division should be done away with altogether. American foreign policy should be kept aboveboard. "When it is deemed vital to legitimate American interests that an Allende go in Chile, let the case be put to Congress. Then, send in the Marines or the airborne." Even the reliably rightist *National Review* agreed that the C.I.A. was out of control. In the columns of that journal, James Burnham, a neoconservative before the term was coined, wrote that the American intelligence system was afflicted by "acute elephantiasis" and needed major restructuring.[3]

Although Congress declined to dismantle the C.I.A., the demands for reform did produce a substantial remodeling. The bars of secrecy were lowered by a new Freedom of Information Act, and many old-timers from the early days of the Cold War were encouraged, sometimes compelled, to find other work. Congressional oversight was reinforced, and assassination as an instrument of American foreign policy was formally disavowed and prohibited.

Specific measures like the War Powers Act and the requirement that the president apprise Congress of covert operations would have a noticeable effect in changing the course of American foreign policy (though not as noticeable as their authors desired), but the most important consequence of the Vietnam War was a fundamental shift in American thinking about the world. From the 1940s to the early 1970s, the prevailing paradigm of American foreign relations was the Munich analogy. World War II had convinced most Americans who thought about such things that if the Western democracies had stood up to Hitler earlier (as at Munich in September 1938, when he demanded the Sudetenland from Czechoslovakia), there might never have been a war. The Munich mindset held that aggression must be opposed wherever it surfaced, even in small, far-off countries that bore little intrinsic importance to the United States. The Munich analogy underpinned the policy of containment, and it motivated the American intervention in Vietnam. As long as the Munich model had produced beneficial results, as in Korea (which most Americans were willing to consider a success, if not an unalloyed one), the American people were willing to stick with it.

[3]H. W. Brands, *The Devil We Knew* (New York, 1993), 138–41.

But the defeat in Vietnam overthrew the Munich mindset and replaced it with another. The lesson of Vietnam was that the United States should stay out of other people's affairs unless there were compelling and undeniable arguments for getting involved. American activities overseas didn't end with the withdrawal of the United States from Vietnam; far from it. American leaders after Vietnam continued to honor earlier commitments, and they made some new ones as well. Yet they were never so free about making or so dead set about honoring such commitments as they had been before Vietnam turned sour. In contrast to the Munich model, under which the burden of proof had been on those who opposed foreign involvement, under the Vietnam version the burden lay with those who advocated it.

2. DETENTE AND ITS DISCONTENTS

Considerably more successful than Nixon's policy toward Vietnam were his policies toward the principal communist powers. From the late 1940s to the late 1960s, American actions in the Cold War had been based on a combination of geopolitics and ideology. Geopolitically, the United States worried about the Soviet Union because the Soviet Union was a great power possessing interests often at variance with American interests, and also possessing the military means to aggressively defend those interests. Briefly: the Soviet Union was big and dangerous, and the United States had to watch out. In this regard the Cold War was no different from other phases of great-power relations since time out of mind.

Ideologically, the United States worried about the Soviet Union because the Soviet Union promoted a belief system—communism—that was antithetical to the democratic capitalism of the United States and its allies. Briefly: the Soviet Union was bent on a world revolution that would overthrow the values and institutions Americans cherished. In this regard the Cold War was something more than an ordinary great-power rivalry. There had been ideological confrontations in the past, as when Islam burst out of the Arabian peninsula in the seventh century and conquered the surrounding regions (the chief ideology in question was of a religious sort but no less ideological for that), and when revolutionary France took on most of the rest of Europe during the 1790s. But the United States had never confronted such an ideological challenge so directly, and for Americans the experience was something new.

Almost from the beginning of the Cold War, a certain tension had existed between the geopolitical aspect of American policy and the ideological aspect, but as long as the communist bloc remained in one piece, the tension didn't prove overwhelming. When the Soviet Union and China fell out with each other during the 1960s, however, geopolitics and ideology began pointing in different directions. Ideology said to continue to treat both communist powers as enemies; geopolitics suggested playing one against the other. A few brave souls had been recommending the latter course for years, but not many people with a chance of gaining responsible office had followed their lead. A false step on the communist question could ruin the career of a budding statesman (or, rarely, stateswoman). Better to leave it alone.

But when Richard Nixon raised the issue of a shift in policy toward the communists, especially the Chinese, serious people began taking notice, not least because, as Washington cynics noted, Nixon was the only one who didn't have to worry about being blindsided by Richard Nixon—the red-baiter par excellence—on the communist question. In a 1967 article in the staidly responsible journal *Foreign Affairs*, he advocated an effort by Washington aimed at "pulling China back into the world community." At this time, though, Nixon was gearing up to challenge Lyndon Johnson—or so he thought—for the presidency, and like many other presidential candidates he saw no advantage in getting too specific on delicate matters. He declined to say just how he would pull China back into the world community after almost twenty years of American efforts to quarantine it.[4]

Nixon became substantially more specific in 1971. In July of that year he unexpectedly announced that he would travel to China to meet with the leaders of that country. Henry Kissinger, the president's national security adviser and later secretary of state, had arranged the forthcoming visit during a confidential mission to Beijing, orchestrated in strictest confidence with the assistance of the president of Pakistan, Agha Yahya Khan. Kissinger feigned an illness of the sort that frequently afflicts travelers; while ostensibly recuperating in the privacy of Yahya's vacation house, he flitted across

---

[4]"Asia after Vietnam," *Foreign Affairs*, October 1967.

Henry Kissinger and Chinese Premier Zhou Enlai are still at arm's-length (and then some) on Kissinger's first trip to China.
Nixon Presidential Materials Project.

the Himalayas to China aboard a special Pakistani plane. The plan almost unraveled when Kissinger contracted a genuine case of gastrointestinal distress in India on the way to Pakistan. "I had to suffer in secret lest I ruin my credibility when we reached Pakistan," Kissinger noted afterward. But he persevered, and the plan succeeded. Shortly after the completion of Kissinger's mission to China, Nixon declared that he would follow. The objective of his visit, he explained, would be "to seek the normalization of relations between the two countries and also to exchange views on questions of concern to the two sides."[5]

Of those questions, none occasioned more concern than the matter of the Soviet Union. For Nixon and Kissinger, normalization with China was chiefly a tactic in American relations with the Soviets. The president and the national security adviser were a strangely matched pair. Each needed the other, and they worked together effectively for more than five years, but they never developed anything like a close personal relationship. Kissinger distrusted

[5]Henry Kissinger, *White House Years* (Boston, 1979), 739; *Public Papers of the Presidents: Nixon,* July 15, 1971.

Nixon—not an unusual attitude, especially in an academic, which Kissinger had been before entering government. "I've hated Nixon for years," Kissinger said in confidence in 1968— before being approached by the Republican nominee for help in formulating foreign policy positions. Kissinger craved power, and Nixon was Kissinger's ticket to power. (If Kissinger had ever harbored any illusions about being elected president in his own right, they vanished on rereading the clause in the Constitution reserving the presidency to natural-born citizens—he had been born in Germany.)[6]

As for Nixon, he recognized Kissinger's obvious abilities. He recognized as well that Kissinger didn't hold him in the highest regard in matters relating to foreign policy. Nixon afterward said that he had heard that "Kissinger had privately made a number of disparaging comments about my competence in the field." But Nixon chose to ignore the comments. He knew that Kissinger shared his fundamental outlook on foreign affairs, and he determined to put Kissinger's capacities to use. At the same time, he always kept a wary eye on his adviser.[7]

The primary feature of the Nixon-Kissinger outlook, the cement that bonded the two men together, was a conviction that geopolitics was the only true currency of international affairs, that ideology was fool's gold and a fool's game. Regarding the communists, Nixon and Kissinger sought to play the Chinese off against the Soviets, to America's advantage. As long as the United States and China had been at swords' points, the Kremlin didn't worry much about a two-front war, against China in the east and NATO in the west. Consequently it could reinforce its military units on the border with China by drawing from units on the Central European front. The rapprochement between Washington and Beijing altered Moscow's calculations. Now collaboration between the Chinese and the Americans appeared entirely too likely. If a crisis developed between the Soviet Union and the United States, and if that crisis reached the point of war, the possibility of having to fight on two fronts could not be ruled out at all. Though Nixon averred that his opening to China was "not directed against any other nation," Soviet leaders couldn't be expected to believe him.[8]

[6]Hersh, *Price of Power*, 14.
[7]Nixon, *Memoirs*, 340.
[8]*Public Papers*, July 15, 1971.

To diminish the possibility of simultaneous trouble with the Americans and the Chinese, the Kremlin sought to lessen tensions with Washington—which was precisely the idea behind Nixon's opening to China. Nixon later gloated: "There were dire predictions that the announcement that I would be going to China, which I made on July 15, 1971, would seriously damage U.S.-Soviet relations. Exactly the opposite occurred." Nixon was right. Moscow agreed to host a summit meeting with Washington, to be held three months after Nixon's visit to China. So anxious, in fact, were the Soviets to talk with the Americans that they chose to overlook Nixon's escalation of bombing attacks against North Vietnam, which included the destruction of four Soviet merchant ships in Haiphong harbor. Moscow's reception crew briefly made as if to roll up the red carpet, but, in the end, left it on the tarmac.[9]

The May 1972 summit meeting between the American president and Soviet general secretary Leonid Brezhnev laid the ground rules for detente. Summarized in a joint statement of twelve "Basic Principles of Relations between the United States of America and the Union of Soviet Socialist Republics," the ground rules asserted, most importantly, each side's adherence to the practice of "peaceful coexistence" despite the differences in ideology that separated the two governments. In other words, capitalists and communists might continue to debate the merits of their respective philosophies of government and political economy, but war—especially in the nuclear age—was not an acceptable rhetorical device. Other basic principles pledged the two governments to avoid actions that might aggravate tensions between them and specifically to attempt to calm regional disputes that otherwise might pull the superpowers toward war. Of lesser importance were several principles involving cultural and scientific exchanges and the details of diplomatic relations.[10]

While skeptics might have been excused for wondering what such vague formulations would translate into in terms of concrete day-to-day dealings between Washington and Moscow, they had less cause to question the importance of two other agreements signed during the Nixon-Brezhnev summit. These two agreements represented a culmination, for the time being at least, of the on-

---

[9]Nixon, *Memoirs*, 522.
[10]*Weekly Compilation of Presidential Documents*, June 5, 1972.

Leonid Brezhnev greets Richard Nixon in Moscow on the trip that codified detente.
Nixon Presidential Materials Project.

going Strategic Arms Limitation Talks (SALT) between the super-powers. The two SALT accords (renamed SALT I after further talks produced a second set of agreements) committed the United States and the Soviet Union to scale back their arms-building plans. Each side would forgo comprehensive antimissile defenses (this part of the deal was often called the A.B.M., for antiballistic missile, treaty), and each would remain below a (rather generous) ceiling of offensive systems.

The 1972 Moscow summit and the agreements it produced formalized detente, which continued to evolve during the next several years. Although considered secondary by Nixon and Kissinger, the economic aspects of detente proved to be the most significant for various influential groups in the United States. American farmers soon came to appreciate the value of the Soviet Union as a market for American grain. So did the railroads, truckers, shipowners, dock-workers, insurance companies, and the myriad other firms and individuals involved in the transactions. While Nixon and Kissinger usually considered themselves to be above such mundane matters as grain sales, they gradually perceived that these sales, and the many others like them that took place as a result of detente, created a constituency for improved relations with the communists among otherwise unlikely groups. Farmers, for instance, had tended to be conservative and staunchly anticommunist, but many decided that good customers might make good neighbors, and they rallied to detente's support.

To the surprise of the Nixon administration and other observers, the Soviets showed themselves to be sharp dealers. During late 1972 and early 1973, they quietly negotiated purchases that essentially cornered the market on surplus American grain. The "great grain robbery," as it was later called, provoked protest among farmers and others connected to the agriculture industry, not because they objected to the principle of the sales but because American farmers received too low a price. American taxpayers objected to the government subsidies that kept the price low for the Soviets and indirectly raised the price of the grain the Kremlin didn't snatch up—and thereby also raised the price of American bread, donuts, breakfast cereal, and pizza. Bumper stickers sprouted proclaiming "Sell Kissinger, not wheat." Yet despite these imperfections in the operation of trade with the Soviets, the commercial side of detente remained its most popular feature.[11]

Detente also gained support from the United States' European allies. For some years, the French and the West Germans had been seeking closer relations with the Soviet Union and the other countries of the Eastern bloc. For the French, a rapprochement with the Soviets signified a lessening of their country's dependence on the United States. Charles de Gaulle, president of France from 1958 to 1969, felt more acutely than most of his compatriots the need to lessen this dependence, but a majority of French men and women sympathized with the overall approach if not always the precise details of his efforts to pull France out from under America's wing, and they backed his attempts to create a single Europe, as he put it, "from the Atlantic to the Urals."

For the Germans, a warming to the East promised both a decrease in the likelihood of war and an increase in the likelihood of maintaining family ties. The West Germans were especially sensitive to the possibility of war, which would probably take place on their

[11]Richard Valeriani, *Travels with Henry* (Boston, 1979), 38.

soil, and which provided the justification for annually annoying NATO maneuvers that churned up their fields, clogged their roads, and shattered their sleep every summer. Additionally, the Germans, more than the people of any other country (except perhaps Vietnam and Korea), felt the divisive effects of the Cold War. Family members caught on opposite sides of the border between West Germany and East Germany had not seen each other for decades. Starting in 1969, the Bonn government of Willy Brandt had initiated its own detente policy under the rubric *Ostpolitik*, and though this policy lacked the global ramifications of the American policy of improving relations with the Soviet Union, it nonetheless provided intellectual and political support for the American policy.

The reaction of other countries to detente was mixed. To many of the governments of Asia, Africa, and Latin America, detente connoted conspiracy between the superpowers. For much of the Cold War, many small countries had tried to keep to a middle ground between the United States and the Soviet Union, in the belief that nonalignment offered the best hope of getting something from each side. Profitable nonalignment, however, depended on active competition between Washington and Moscow, each of which would shower benevolence on the third countries out of fear that those countries would line up with the other side. An easing of the rivalry between the superpowers threatened to curtail the largesse the superpowers were willing to dispense for air bases, port facilities, electronic listening posts, votes at the United Nations, and the like.

No country felt the danger of detente more acutely than North Vietnam. Hanoi's leaders were justified in their fear, for a major objective of detente as envisioned by Nixon and Kissinger was to cut off communist aid to North Vietnam. The White House hoped that by dangling the promise of improved relations with the United States in front of each of the two major communist powers, as well as by brandishing the implicit threat of collaboration with each against the other, it might persuade Beijing and Moscow to pressure Hanoi to accept reasonable terms for an American withdrawal from Vietnam. Pressure from outside had worked before: at the 1954 Geneva conference that had originally divided Vietnam (temporarily, or so it was decreed), the Soviets and Chinese had browbeaten Ho Chi Minh and his Vietminh comrades into accepting less from France than they thought they had won on the battlefield. Moscow at the time was attempting an early and very tentative version of detente, with Stalin's emergent successors seeking to engage the Americans in dialogue, and a Vietnamese settlement that was relatively generous to the West seemed likely to further the rapprochement. (It did, to the extent of facilitating the first superpower summit in ten years, at Geneva in 1955.) But the Vietnamese communists felt cheated. "We were betrayed," declared Pham Van Dong, the chief Vietminh negotiator at Geneva and the North Vietnamese prime minister throughout the war against the Americans. Though Ho Chi Minh died in 1969, Pham and his colleagues wanted no part of a repetition of the betrayal.[12]

Yet they recognized that they might not have a choice. China and the Soviet Union supplied most of North Vietnam's military equipment, and if those two powers interrupted the flow of arms, Hanoi would be hard-pressed to keep its army, now on the verge of victory, active in the field. For this reason, the North Vietnamese government looked with deepest distrust on the whole idea of detente. Hanoi's official newspaper castigated Washington for seeking a "balance of the great powers" that would "give United States imperialism complete freedom of action" in crushing the world revolutionary movement, especially "the patriotic struggle of the people of the Indochina peninsula." That the imperialists of the West should attempt such a maneuver was not exactly shocking, but that the socialists of the East would participate in such a plot was. Hanoi's editor blasted Moscow and Beijing for "bogging down on the dark, muddy road of compromise" and for giving preference to "peaceful coexistence over proletarian internationalism, serving their own immediate interests at the expense of the revolutionary movement." Hoping to stiffen spines on the central committees of Hanoi's two allies, the editor asserted, "We Communists must persist in revolution and should not compromise."[13]

Though the North Vietnamese were prudent to worry, as matters worked out Moscow and Beijing brought only modest pressure to bear against Hanoi, and to little effect. The Soviets and Chinese had their own credibility to conserve, and neither desired to be seen as selling an ally down the river. For their part, the North Vietnamese were too close to victory to accept any settlement that might permanently damage their chances of reunifying Vietnam. Hanoi

---

[12]*New York Times Magazine,* June 24, 1990.
[13]Raymond L. Garthoff, *Detente and Confrontation* (Washington, 1985), 259.

did agree in the 1973 Paris accords to suspend fighting, but to almost no one's surprise the suspension turned out to be temporary.

Ironically, while detente was designed to extricate the United States from Vietnam, it was subsequently cited as a reason for the United States to get involved in other Third World wars. The most controversial of these occurred in Angola. Fighting there broke out following a sequence of tumultuous events in Portugal, the colonial master of Angola, that overturned an authoritarian rightist regime in Lisbon and replaced it with a more moderate representative government. Portugal's new rulers soon proclaimed the independence of their country's African colonies, including Angola. As independence approached, various factions within Angola jockeyed for position. The principal contenders were the Popular Movement for the Liberation of Angola (M.P.L.A.), the Front for the National Liberation of Angola (F.N.L.A.), and the National Union for the Total Independence of Angola (UNITA). Ideology separated the contenders, with the M.P.L.A. being more radical than the F.N.L.A. and UNITA, but tribal affinities and the personal ambitions of each group's leaders were equally important in sparking the struggle. Once the fighting got going, the three groups received outside support, which tended to polarize the situation further. The Soviet Union and Cuba underwrote the activities of the M.P.L.A., while the United States covertly subsidized the F.N.L.A. The F.N.L.A. also received assistance from the government of Mobutu Sese Seko of Zaire, a longtime American client. To complicate matters, China sent arms and advisers to the F.N.L.A. as well. When UNITA joined forces with the F.N.L.A. against the M.P.L.A., UNITA began receiving assistance from the United States and China. To complicate matters still more, South Africa dispatched military units to bolster the F.N.L.A.-UNITA alliance.

The implications of the Angolan war for detente weren't clear at first. The Moscow basic principles seemed to say that Washington and Moscow should be cooperating to pacify the situation in Angola rather than inflaming it by arming the opposing sides. That the Moscow principles weren't being applied to Angola suggested to some critics the limitations of detente. The Kremlin might talk about peaceful coexistence, these critics said, but Moscow's agents were as hard at work as ever trying to spread communism.

The White House and the State Department understood the vulnerability of detente to this kind of criticism. By the time the Angolan war broke out, Nixon had resigned the presidency, but Kissinger remained in office. Gerald Ford had never pretended to be an expert on international affairs (many considered him an expert on nothing at all; Lyndon Johnson unkindly and partisanly once said of the Republican former footballer that he had played too many games without his helmet). Ford didn't begin pretending to be a foreign affairs expert now, instead deferring to Kissinger on all matters of substance in foreign relations. Kissinger thrived on recognition of his expertise and power. When he was appointed secretary of state, a reporter asked him what he wished to be called—Mr. Secretary or Dr. Secretary. "Just call me 'Excellency,'" Kissinger replied. He was joking, but only half joking. During the Nixon presidency Kissinger had spent much of his time undercutting, dead-ending, and otherwise diminishing his rivals in the administration. Now, under Ford, he didn't have any rivals.[14]

Kissinger considered the Angolan conflict a test of detente. As a geopolitician as well as a student of nineteenth-century European diplomacy, Kissinger recognized that competition among great powers was natural and inevitable. Just because Washington and Moscow had taken steps to render their competition somewhat safer was no reason to think that the competition would end. The Soviet Union was watching to see whether the United States after Vietnam possessed the will to continue the competition. The Americans must demonstrate that they did. If they failed to do so, the Kremlin would feel free to ignore its other pledges. Detente might soon be rendered meaningless.

Congress perceived the situation differently. In the wake of Vietnam, aid to Angolan guerrillas was a tough sell. When Kissinger and Ford asked the legislature in November 1975 for additional covert funding for Angola, many members—especially Democrats—refused to stand by while the executive branch entangled the United States in another distant civil war. In the Senate, Birch Bayh rebuked the White House for not paying attention to recent history. "Despite the tragic and bitter lessons we should have learned from our intervention in civil war in Southeast Asia," Bayh declared, "the Ford administration persists in deepening our involvement in the civil strife in Angola." The Indiana Democrat continued, "The war in Angola

[14]Valeriani, *Travels with Henry,* 7.

presents the first test of American foreign policy after Vietnam. Unfortunately, our performance to date indicates that we have not learned from our mistakes. Rather than recognizing our limitations and carefully analyzing our interests, we are again plunging into a conflict in a far corner of the world as if we believed it was still our mission to serve as policeman of the world." Thomas Eagleton of Missouri asked, "Is it sound policy to become embroiled in an African war? Is it wise to ally ourselves in this venture, even indirectly, with South Africa?" Eagleton made clear that he thought not. Robert Byrd of West Virginia predicted that associating with South Africa could spell "disaster" for American relations with Africa and much of the Third World. Edward Kennedy turned the old domino theory on its head and applied it specifically to covert operations. "If ever there is a 'domino effect,'" Kennedy asserted, "it is how covert activities can easily fall into overt involvement and long-term commitments." The Massachusetts senator added, "The American people will not tolerate this. The United States must avoid this in Angola."[15]

When Senators Dick Clark and John Tunney introduced an amendment effectively barring covert aid for Angola, the Ford administration opposed the measure, but to no avail. It was the administration's bad luck that congressional assertiveness regarding foreign affairs reached an apex during this period, the result both of legislative indignation regarding Vietnam and Watergate and of executive enervation consequent to the Nixon disgrace and resignation. A stronger president than Ford might have made a major issue of aid for Angola, but Ford confined himself to warning that the decision to cut off aid was "a deep tragedy for all countries whose security depends on the United States" and that "responsibilities abandoned today will return as more acute crises tomorrow." Anticipating a veto override, the president signed the bill containing the aid ban into law.[16]

Perhaps partly as a result of the suspension of American aid, but more fundamentally as a result of developments on the ground in Angola, the leftist M.P.L.A. won the first round of the Angolan civil war. (Subsequent rounds would continue into the mid-1990s.) The M.P.L.A. victory played into the hands of groups that opposed

---

[15]*Congressional Record*, Dec. 15–19, 1975.
[16]Department of State *Bulletin*, Jan. 19, 1976.

detente. Such groups had existed from the moment Nixon announced that he was going to Beijing, but initially they had experienced difficulty in formulating a case for their opposition. The fact that Dick Nixon, the Kremlin-basher from the early days of the Cold War, was the designer of detente preemptively spiked the guns of many critics. If Nixon thought it was okay to talk to the commies, who were these critics to carp? Gradually the critics regained their voices, but with the memories of Vietnam still painfully fresh in America, they couldn't summon a majority to follow their advice regarding aid for Angola.

All the same, the M.P.L.A. triumph added to the burdens detente had to carry. When Watergate had discredited Nixon, it also damaged detente. Not only did the disgrace of detente's chief sponsor reflect badly on his policies, but it left detente in the care of Gerald Ford and Henry Kissinger, neither of whom possessed the stature among conservatives that had rendered Nixon largely invulnerable to allegations of softness against communism. Detente's denigrators lashed out at Kissinger, especially, with a zest they couldn't summon for Nixon. A spokesman for the increasingly influential Committee on the Present Danger offered one of the kinder comments when he called Kissinger's policies "very shortranged" and charged that they did more for Kissinger's personal popularity than for the interests of the United States. A more forthright critic pronounced Kissinger "a traitor to his country."[17]

Despite the troubles that developed in implementing detente, in principle the Nixon-Kissinger policy of relaxation toward the communists was the most creative approach to U.S. foreign relations since the early years of the Cold War. By detaching ideology from geopolitics—which detaching was the essence of detente—Nixon and Kissinger allowed the United States the maneuvering room it required in an increasingly complex world. They rejected the reflexive anticommunism that had characterized American policy for two decades, substituting instead a pragmatic pursuit of mutual benefit with Moscow and Beijing.

Nixon and Kissinger weren't so naive as to think that mutual benefit covered all or even most areas of relations between the United States and the communists, and they realized that the Sovi-

---

[17]Robert D. Schulzinger, *Henry Kissinger* (New York, 1989), 220–21; Brands, *Devil We Knew*, 153.

ets and the Chinese would continue to seek their own advantage wherever they could. But the two men deemed such advantage-seeking normal and manageable. They thought they could protect American interests better by looking on the communists as circumstantial competitors rather than existential enemies, as ordinarily ambitious rather than implacably evil.

3. MONEY TALKS

While Nixon's and Kissinger's embrace of detente indicated that political realities among the great powers had changed since the 1940s, simultaneous developments in another area demonstrated that economic realities had changed no less. For the quarter century after World War II, the structure of international finance had rested on a foundation of American dollars. The war had ended with Americans owning roughly half the industrial output of the planet and considerably more than half of the world's mobilizable wealth. At the 1944 Bretton Woods conference and elsewhere afterward, American leaders parlayed their economic advantage into favorable terms of post-war trade and investment. Via the World Bank and the International Monetary Fund (I.M.F.), both of which the United States controlled by virtue of being the majority shareholder, Washington encouraged the opening up of foreign markets to American goods and capital. The General Agreement on Tariffs and Trade (GATT), though not quite so clearly controlled by the United States, even more explicitly codified the free-market principles that American officials judged essential to American prosperity and world peace. Undergirding the whole arrangement was a scheme of fixed exchange rates that pegged the other major currencies to the dollar. Along with the great size of America's economy relative to the economies of its trading partners, this effectively made the dollar a single world currency. Finally, the Bretton Woods system fixed the dollar against gold at thirty-five dollars per ounce.

The Bretton Woods financial framework functioned well for two decades, but by the end of that period strains were starting to develop. The source of the strains was the fact that the United States no longer dominated the world economy as it had during the late 1940s. Japan and Germany, which had been thoroughly flattened by the war, were now up and about and growing stronger fast. As

Americans and inhabitants of other countries purchased products made in Japan or Germany, they demanded yen and deutschemarks to pay for their purchases. The growing demand for those currencies put pressure on the fixed exchange rates of the Bretton Woods system. As international merchants and money managers found the dollar comparatively less attractive than it had been, some sought the refuge of gold, exchanging their dollars for bullion from the American gold reserve. Partly as a consequence of these international developments, and partly from domestic causes—notably the requirements of funding both Lyndon Johnson's Great Society and the war in Vietnam—inflation became an increasing problem in the United States. As price levels in the United States rose, budgets (both governmental and household) felt the pinch. The pinching created political pressure that by the early 1970s forced the Nixon administration to take action to alleviate the pain.

In August 1971 Nixon announced a bold new policy. The president unilaterally abrogated the system of fixed exchange rates by suspending the dollar's official convertibility into other currencies, and he closed the American "gold window" by suspending government sales of gold. At the same time, he established wage and price controls, imposed a 10 percent surcharge on imports, and slashed federal taxes and spending.

In terms of symbolic value, the most important of these actions were the abrogation of the fixed-rate system and the closing of the gold window. The two measures amounted to an admission that the American economy no longer ruled the world economy and that the United States could no longer call the tune other nations' economies danced to. The dollar was far from obsolete, if only because there were so many dollars in circulation throughout the world. Yet it was also far from omnipotent, as it had sometimes seemed to be.

Nixon's new policy momentarily eased both domestic inflation and the international pressure on the dollar, but because the underlying transformation of the world economy—in particular, the growing strength of other countries relative to the United States—continued apace, the pressure eventually built up again. At a series of meetings commencing in late 1971 and lasting into the mid-1970s, the finance ministers of the major industrial countries devised various measures to restore stability to international financial markets. Some of the measures succeeded better than others, but none proved generally satisfactory until a March 1973 agreement by the governments of the industrial countries to switch to a system of floating exchange rates. Under this arrangement, the relative values of the different currencies would be determined by the law of supply and demand. The dollar, the yen, the mark, the pound, the franc, and so on would be commodities much like any others, with their prices reflecting the desire of people and institutions to possess them.

The system of floating exchange rates took a bit of getting used to. Even Nixon's treasury secretary, George Shultz, an economist by training who on the whole supported floating rates, suggested that some kind of fixed schedule ought to be the "center of gravity" around which the floating rates moved. Merchants and investors who operated internationally now had to factor the uncertainty of shifting exchange rates into their projections. Would the dollar rise or fall against other currencies during the course of a transaction or the lifetime of an investment? The answer to this question could make all the difference in determining whether to attempt a sale, start a new business, or expand an old one.[18]

The disintegration of the Bretton Woods system and the introduction of floating exchange rates had mixed consequences for Americans. The principal immediate effect of the new financial regime was the devaluation of the dollar relative to other currencies. While devaluation made life more difficult and expensive for Americans traveling overseas and made imports more costly, it enhanced the competitive position of American exporters. In doing so it improved America's balance of payments, strengthened the profits of export firms, and increased employment therein.

At the same time, though, the adoption of floating exchange rates provided additional evidence of America's decline relative to other countries. After 1973 the dollar was an ordinary currency. It could rise and fall just like other currencies. As things happened, as a result of the stresses that had finally broken the Bretton Woods system, the dollar fell more often than it rose. Consequently, even while the American evacuation of South Vietnam signaled the end of an era in American diplomatic and military policy, the abandonment of the Bretton Woods system marked the end of an era in American economic policy.

[18]Robert Solomon, *The International Monetary System, 1945–1981* (New York, 1982), 334.

4. OLD ENEMIES . . .

As investors, speculators, bankers, and merchants were getting used to the new system of floating exchange rates, events of the final months of 1973 gave them something else to get used to. In October 1973 a fourth installment of the Arab-Israeli war broke out, causing the expected flutters in the foreign ministries of the great powers, more than the expected flutters in the defense ministries of the superpowers, and convulsions in the finance ministries of the countries that purchased petroleum.

In certain respects, the October War of 1973 (also called the Yom Kippur War, from the fact that it began on the Jewish holy day) was a consequence of detente. In the same way that the leadership of North Vietnam worried that good feeling between Washington and the big communist states would result in pressure to modify Hanoi's agenda, so the Egyptian government of Anwar el-Sadat worried that detente would impede the accomplishment of Egypt's objectives. In particular, President Sadat feared that rapprochement between the United States and the Soviet Union would remove an important incentive for the Americans to lean on Israel to return the territory it had won from Egypt, Syria, and Jordan during the 1967 June (Six Day) War. Sadat and other Arab leaders recognized the powerful influences that operated in the United States on behalf of Israel, and they understood that the chief countervailing influence was concern that further conflict in the Middle East might mushroom into something larger and more dangerous, perhaps even a confrontation with the Soviet Union. Detente threatened to remove the danger of a broader conflict, and in doing so threatened to diminish the desire of the American government to force Israel to give up the occupied territories, including Egypt's Sinai Peninsula. In addition, detente would incline the Soviets to please the Americans rather than the Egyptians, whom Moscow had supplied with money and weapons for almost twenty years.

Not long after the detente-defining Moscow summit, Sadat began thinking of making his move before the superpowers got even chummier than they were. In part to register his disapproval of the Kremlin's embrace of detente, especially as it apparently was diminishing Moscow's desire to support Egypt's efforts to regain the Sinai, Sadat sent the more than fifteen thousand Soviet military advisers in Egypt packing. At the same time, he took steps to improve relations with the United States, which had long been strained on account of the American support for Israel. Most portentously, the Egyptian president laid plans for an attack on Israeli positions in the Sinai and elsewhere. At the beginning of 1973, he authorized the creation of a joint military command with Syria, which shared Egypt's desire to reopen the war against Israel. Over the next several months, the officers of this command developed plans for an assault against Israel. Egyptian troops would invade the Sinai across the Suez Canal, while Syrian units would scale the eastern slope of the Golan Heights. Careful timing on the part of the Arabs would force the Israelis to fight a two-front war, and the Arabs would stand a reasonable chance of winning back at least some of the territory they had lost. Equally important, Arab fighters would win back the honor and respect they had lost in their ignominious defeat by the Israelis in the 1967 war.

Because the Israelis were overconfident after their smashing victory in that earlier war, they paid comparatively little attention to the Egyptian-Syrian preparations for battle, which were disguised as mundane military maneuvers. In addition, Arab commandos created a diversion by hijacking a train in Austria carrying Soviet Jews bound for Israel and perhaps the occupied West Bank. The ensuing hostage drama mesmerized the Israeli government and pulled the attention of Israel's people away from Egypt and Syria. Israel's intelligence service dismissed the activities of the Egyptians and Syrians as insignificant. "We consider the opening of military operations against Israel by the two armies as of low probability," the Israeli analysts said. The C.I.A., basing its judgment largely on the confidence of the Israelis, agreed: "The military preparations that have occurred do not indicate that any party intends to initiate hostilities."[19]

Both the Israelis and the C.I.A. were wrong. On October 6, Egyptian units threw pontoon bridges across the Suez Canal and attacked Israeli defenses on the eastern bank. Egyptian soldiers blasted sandbagged Israeli positions with water cannons, breaching the lines and opening the way for Egyptian troops to penetrate. Egyptian armor sliced past Israeli positions and raced for the strategic Mitla and Gidi passes in the Sinai interior. Meanwhile Syrian soldiers mounted an assault on the Israeli forces in the Golan Heights. Paratroops landed on the slopes of Mount Hermon, and infantry

[19]Henry Kissinger, *Years of Upheaval* (Boston, 1982), 465–66.

drove upward from Damascus. The Syrian soldiers broke through the Israeli lines and thrust almost to the Israeli-Syrian border.

These early reverses didn't particularly alarm the Israeli high command. The setbacks occurred in the occupied territories rather than in Israel itself (which confirmed to many Israelis the wisdom of having held on to the territories), and the Israelis fully expected to be able to mount successful counteroffensives. "It is our intention to throw every last Syrian and Egyptian back behind the ceasefire lines," Prime Minister Golda Meir's office informed Israeli foreign minister Abba Eban at the United Nations on the first day of the war. Israeli troops began putting this intention into effect within forty-eight hours, and before long they were inflicting serious damage on their attackers.[20]

Yet even though the early phase of fighting didn't directly threaten Israel's security, the losses incurred by Israeli forces in re-pelling the attacks stunned the Israeli people. More than five hun-dred Israeli soldiers were killed, a small number by the standards of most wars but many more than Israel had ever suffered in a compa-rable period. In addition, Israel lost one hundred airplanes and five hundred tanks. The net result was a grave blow to Israeli morale and a potentially serious erosion of Israel's fighting capacity.

This result was what pulled the United States into the war. Washington obviously couldn't bring the dead Israeli soldiers back to life, but it could resupply Israel's arsenal. The Israeli gov-ernment frantically requested that a resupply operation begin at once. The Israelis benefited from the fact that this time, unlike the 1967 war, they had not launched the initial attack. That they had been attacked made it easier for the Nixon administration to ap-prove the Israeli request than otherwise would have been the case. The Israelis contended that they were the victims of unprovoked ag-gression, and they demanded that the United States stand by previ-ous pledges to come to Israel's aid if Israel ever needed it. (The Arabs had a different interpretation of the aggression issue, pointing out that when Egypt invaded the Sinai and Syria the Golan Heights, those two countries were merely trying to reclaim territory illegally held by Israel.)

The Nixon administration was willing enough to send Israel the

---

[20]Matti Golan, *The Secret Conversations of Henry Kissinger* (trans. by Ruth Geyra Stern and Sol Stern: New York, 1976), 63.

weapons it wanted. As early as the afternoon of the first day of fighting, Kissinger told the Israeli ambassador that the White House would "almost certainly approve" reasonable requests for rearmament. The secretary of state added that if the Soviets started shipping weapons to Egypt and Syria, "then we will certainly do it."[21]

But the administration preferred to keep the Israelis a little off balance. As the tide of battle turned in Israel's favor, Nixon and Kissinger desired to avoid a repetition of 1967, when the Israelis had thoroughly thrashed the Arabs. If the Israelis won big again, they would set the possibility of a genuine peace settlement back at least a decade. The Israelis didn't help their case when one of their diplomats boasted to Kissinger that in a few days the prewar lines would look very attractive to the Egyptians and the Syrians. For Washington, a battlefield draw would be much better. "We want the fighting to end on a basis where we can build a lasting peace," Nixon stated. The president later elaborated on his strategy: "I believed that only a battlefield stalemate would provide the foundation in which fruitful negotiations might begin. Any equilibrium, even if only an equilibrium of mutual exhaustion, would make it easier to reach an enforceable settlement."[22]

To keep the Israelis from racking up another thumping victory, the Nixon administration rationed its resupply of the Israeli forces. Initially it required the Israelis themselves to pick up the weapons from American military bases, and it insisted that they do so in unmarked planes. Whether this maneuver actually fooled anyone is hard to say, but it averted the possibility that Israeli planes would be photographed taking off from American bases. Because Israel was not a formal American ally, and because the United States government liked to profess evenhandedness between the Arabs and Israel, such photographs would have been embarrassing.

Yet the administration soon lost its sensitivity to embarrassment of this sort. As the course of the fighting turned against the Egyptians and Syrians, the Arabs looked to the Soviet Union for resupply operations of their own. The Kremlin decided to ignore Sadat's brusque treatment of the Soviet advisers and to forgive sundry other affronts, and began airlifting weapons to Egypt and Syria.

[21]Kissinger, *Years of Upheaval*, 479.
[22]William B. Quandt, *Decade of Decisions* (Berkeley, 1977), 187 n. ; Nixon, *Memoirs*, 921.

The Nixon administration interpreted this Soviet intervention as both a threat to Israel and a challenge to detente. Kissinger explained the American position: "Our policy with respect to detente is clear: We shall resist aggressive foreign policies. Detente cannot survive irresponsibility in any area, including the Middle East." Beyond verbal warnings, the administration stepped up its resupply operation to the Israelis. The administration ordered American cargo planes to deliver weapons and ammunition directly to Israel. Soon the American airlift was landing a thousand tons of supplies per day at Israeli bases. Included among these supplies were top-of-the-line American fighter-bombers.[23]

The appearance of all the American weapons restored Israel's confidence—too much so for Washington's taste, as matters soon proved. No longer having to conserve rifle bullets and tank engines, the Israelis threw their forces unstintingly against the Egyptian and Syrian positions. In the south, the Israelis drove far across the Suez Canal into Egypt proper, where they surrounded and threatened to annihilate the Egyptian Third Army. In the north, Israeli troops pummeled the Syrians, pushed them back down the mountains, and headed for Damascus.

At this stage, the Nixon administration decided to press for a cease-fire. The Israelis had proved their point that the Arabs mustn't try anything like the recent attack again, and Nixon and Kissinger wanted to stop the fighting before the Israelis captured a lot of new territory. Until this juncture, both the United States and the Soviet Union had publicly proclaimed their devotion to a peaceful and swift resolution of the fighting, yet thus far they had failed to coordinate their efforts to achieve such an outcome. Instead they had concentrated on demonstrating their resolve against each other by supplying weapons to their respective clients. But after two weeks of fighting, Washington and Moscow came to perceive the wisdom of ending the war before it jeopardized detente.

On October 20 Kissinger flew to Moscow. There he and Brezhnev engaged in a moderate amount of blustering about the grave dangers inherent in a failure to stem the fighting (on terms favorable to their own countries, of course) before agreeing to work together in the interests of peace.

Kissinger might have blustered more convincingly but for the

---

[23]Kissinger, *Years of Upheaval*, 491.

fact that the Nixon administration was imploding in Washington at the very time the secretary of state was negotiating in Moscow. When Kissinger telephoned White House chief of staff Alexander Haig to relay the latest Soviet offer, Haig responded that he had other things on his mind than the Middle East. Kissinger inquired as to what could be more important than peace between the Arabs and Israelis. Haig replied that Nixon had just fired the Watergate special prosecutor, setting in motion a chain of events promptly labeled the "Saturday night massacre." As Haig summarized, "All hell has broken loose." Kissinger judged that a swift settlement of the war in the Middle East was now more imperative than ever. The confusion in Washington might tempt the Soviets to rash action.[24]

From Moscow, Kissinger flew to Israel to persuade the government there to accept a cease-fire. Prime Minister Meir had been on

[24]Ibid., 552.

A skeptical Golda Meir listens to Richard Nixon deliver his thoughts on the Middle East.
Nixon Presidential Materials Project.

reasonably good terms with Nixon and Kissinger. On an earlier visit to Washington, she had expressed some concern regarding the Nixon administration's moves toward detente. Were Americans perhaps dropping their guard prematurely? Nixon replied that his eyes were wide open. "Our Golden Rule as far as international diplomacy is concerned is: 'Do unto others as they do unto you.'" To which Kissinger added, "Plus ten percent." Meir smiled. "As long as you approach things that way," she said, "we have no fears." On another occasion, Nixon was making small talk with the Israeli leader. Nixon was never very good in such circumstances, and he was struggling to find something the two of them had in common. "We both have Jewish foreign ministers," he finally blurted out. Meir, mentally comparing the urbane, multilingual Abba Eban to the heavily accented Kissinger, responded, "Yes, but mine speaks English without an accent." (Kissinger's accent was legendary. His aides never could keep from laughing when he discussed negotiations for an international Law of the Seas; from Kissinger's mouth it came out Law of Disease.)[25]

Despite their generally cooperative relationship with Washington, Meir and her associates were skeptical when Kissinger arrived in October 1973. The secretary of state found them surprisingly unsure of themselves, notwithstanding the military victories they were achieving. "Deep down," Kissinger wrote afterward, "the Israelis knew that while they had won the last battle, they had lost the aura of invincibility. The Arab armies were not destroyed. The Arab nations had not won, but no longer need they quail before Israeli might. Israel, after barely escaping disaster, had prevailed militarily; it ended up with more Arab territory captured than lost. But it was entering an uncertain and lonely future, dependent on a shrinking circle of friends." Like the leaders of North Vietnam and Egypt, Meir suspected the Americans and Soviets of detente-inspired collusion. In particular she fretted that Kissinger and Brezhnev had agreed to push Israel back to its pre-1967 borders. She demanded of Kissinger whether this was the case. Kissinger assured her that it was not. Meir then demanded to know what other borders the superpowers were planning to impose on Israel. Kissinger said there was no such plan. Meir's questions confirmed Kissinger's assessment of Israel's psychological vulnerability. "As she explored all possible permuta-

---

[25]Nixon, *Memoirs*, 478; Valeriani, *Travels with Henry*, 10.

tions of American duplicity, she exemplified the enormous insecurity inherent in Israel's geographic and demographic position and its total dependence on the United States."[26]

Perhaps Meir intentionally overstated Israel's worries, as a bargaining tactic. If so, it worked, for while accepting the basic idea of a cease-fire, Meir and her generals persuaded Kissinger to allow Israel a certain amount of leeway in meeting the deadline for the cease-fire. When one of Israel's commanders claimed that completing his forces' work on the southern front would require only two or three days more, Kissinger responded, "Two or three days? That's all? Well, in Vietnam the ceasefire didn't go into effect at the exact time that was agreed on." The Egyptians and Syrians were more than ready to call the fighting off, and, now assured that Washington would look the other way regarding last-minute operations, the Israelis likewise consented to stop shooting.[27]

The cease-fire had hardly taken effect, however, before it started fraying. Each side accused the other of violating the truce, and soon artillery salvos accompanied the accusations. Within hours the war had resumed in full force.

Fighting in the Middle East has always worried Washington, but the failure of the 1973 cease-fire was particularly worrisome in that it suggested that the affairs of the region were spinning out of control. They seemed about to spin even faster when Moscow called for the deployment of a combined Soviet-American peacekeeping force. Brezhnev asserted his hope that the United States would accept this proposal, but he went on to declare that if Washington couldn't see its way to concur in the plan, Moscow would have to move on its own. "I will say it straight," Brezhnev told Nixon, "that if you find it impossible to act with us in this matter, we should be faced with the necessity urgently to consider the question of taking appropriate steps unilaterally." To demonstrate his government's seriousness, Brezhnev placed several airborne divisions on alert and ordered the Soviet Mediterranean fleet to prepare for action.[28]

The Nixon administration vehemently rejected the idea of Soviet troops in the Middle East, whether in the company of American forces or otherwise. Ever since 1945, the U.S. government had taken

[26]Kissinger, *Years of Upheaval*, 561–64.
[27]Golan, *Secret Conversations*, 86.
[28]Kissinger, *Years of Upheaval*, 583.

great pains to keep the Red Army out of the Middle East, and Nixon and Kissinger had no intention of altering that policy. Once the Soviets entered the region, even as peacekeepers, there might be no getting them out. Despite Nixon's Watergate troubles, the president told Brezhnev to drop his plan to send troops, or else. He said that the Kremlin's plan was "not appropriate in the present circumstances" and that the United States could view the general secretary's intimations of unilateral action only as "a matter of the gravest concern involving incalculable consequences." Nixon lent weight to his remarks by going Brezhnev one better in the game of huffing and puffing: he placed American conventional and nuclear forces around the world on alert.[29]

Many Nixon watchers at this time suspected that he was overreacting to events in the Middle East for the sake of his domestic political position, which was crumbling by the hour. There may have been something to this suspicion. Nixon himself toyed with what he called the "madman" approach to superpower relations, which involved his deliberately fostering the impression that he was mentally unbalanced and, because his finger rested on the nuclear trigger, had to be given a wide berth.[30]

Whatever the merits of the madman policy, or of the suspicions of the Nixon-phobes, by his strong language and the highly visible bustling about on American military bases (high visibility was the point: no effort was made to conceal the preparations for war) Nixon caused the Kremlin to postpone whatever plans it had for sending troops to the Middle East.

To convert the postponement into a cancellation, the administration intensified its pressure on the Israelis to put down their weapons. Not only did continued fighting in the Middle East endanger detente, it reflected poorly on the United States. Kissinger afterward explained, "If the United States held still while the Egyptian army was being destroyed after an American sponsored ceasefire and a Secretary of State's visit to Israel, not even the most moderate Arab could cooperate with us any longer."[31]

The Israelis got the message. Following some final consolidation of their military position, they agreed to put down their rifles,

[29]Nixon, *Memoirs*, 939.
[30]Hersh, *Price of Power*, 53.
[31]Kissinger, *Years of Upheaval*, 571.

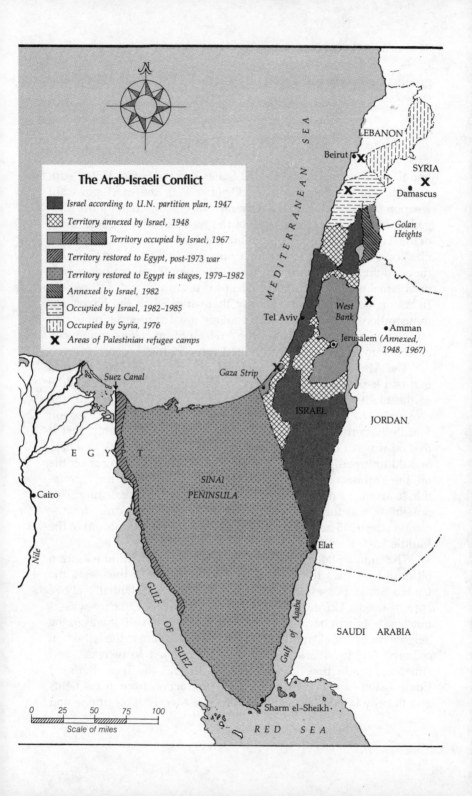

The Arab-Israeli Conflict

- **Israel according to U.N. partition plan, 1947**
- **Territory annexed by Israel, 1948**
- **Territory occupied by Israel, 1967**
- **Territory restored to Egypt, post-1973 war**
- **Territory restored to Egypt in stages, 1979–1982**
- **Annexed by Israel, 1982**
- **Occupied by Israel, 1982–1985**
- **Occupied by Syria, 1976**
- **X** Areas of Palestinian refugee camps

LEBANON

Beirut

SYRIA

Damascus

Golan
Heights

MEDITERRANEAN SEA

West
Bank

Tel Aviv

Amman

Jerusalem (*Annexed,
1948, 1967*)

Gaza Strip

ISRAEL

JORDAN

Suez Canal

E G Y P T

SINAI
PENINSULA

Cairo

Nile

GULF OF SUEZ

Elat

Gulf of Aqaba

SAUDI   ARABIA

Sharm el–Sheikh

| 0 | 25 | 50 | 75 | 100 |
Scale of miles

RED   SEA

ground their planes, and shut off their tanks. On October 27 the war ended.

5. ... NEW WEAPONS

For all the armaments the United States and the Soviet Union supplied to the combatants in the October War, the most powerful weapon unveiled during the fighting was of a different nature altogether. During the second week of the war, just after the beginning of the American resupply operation, the Arab members of the Organization of Petroleum Exporting Countries (OPEC) announced that they would reduce petroleum production by 5 percent per month until Israel withdrew from the occupied territories and restored the rights of the Palestinians. Shortly thereafter, when the Nixon administration requested a special congressional appropriation to pay for the material going to Israel, the Arab OPEC members announced an embargo on oil shipments to the United States.

The Arab oil embargo threatened to produce the kind of crisis that had kept American strategists staring at ceilings in the middle of the night for twenty-five years. Ever since World War II, the economies of America's West European allies had depended on Middle Eastern oil. American officials worried, reasonably, that if that oil was cut off, those economies would quickly clank to a halt. Should unfriendly persons or groups merely threaten to cut off the oil, the Europeans would find it very difficult to resist the temptation to arrange a deal with whoever was doing the threatening. This possibility was the principal reason that every American administration after 1945 had taken such pains to keep the Soviets out of the Middle East.

The United States itself hadn't gotten hooked on Middle Eastern oil until later than the Europeans. Through most of the 1960s, the United States possessed production potential substantially above current needs. During the early 1960s the excess capacity was as much as 4 million barrels per day, while as late as 1970 it was in the neighborhood of 1 million barrels. But thereafter the situation changed rapidly. Worldwide demand continued to increase, and American production began to tail off. In 1971 the Texas Railroad Commission—the body that dictated production from Texas fields and thereby largely determined domestic American oil prices, and until recently had strongly influenced world prices—authorized production at 100 percent of capacity for the first time since World War II. "We feel this to be an historic occasion," the chairman of the Texas commission declared. "Damned historic, and a sad one. Texas oil fields have been like a reliable old warrior that could rise to the task when needed. That old warrior can't rise anymore."[32]

As the world petroleum market stretched tight, oil-producing nations found themselves enjoying unprecedented power. Particularly powerful were countries like Saudi Arabia that produced far more than they consumed. The Saudis, and to a lesser extent the other Middle Eastern producers, could easily adjust production to suit market conditions. If the price was high, they could pump rivers of oil and make mountains of money. If the price was low, they could leave the oil in the ground and wait until prices rose.

This flexibility in production was what had led to the establishment of OPEC in 1960, but for a decade the cartel struck no terror into the hearts of consuming countries or their governments. As long as big consumers like the United States had excess production capacity, the scope for manipulation of supplies and prices was limited. But as the slack in the world oil market vanished during the early 1970s, OPEC suddenly became formidable. Prices climbed upward during the first years of the new decade, and when the OPEC delegates gathered in Vienna in the autumn of 1973, they planned to push prices higher still.

As luck (the producers' good luck, consumers' bad luck) would have it, the October War broke out in the Middle East at just this time. Fighting in the Middle East always drove oil prices up, as consumers feared damage to the oil fields, shippers worried about the safety of their ships, insurers demanded wartime premiums, and speculators purchased all the oil they could get their hands on. The October War added the political dimension of Arab hostility toward the United States, which led to the Arab oil embargo and the announced production cuts. Under the combined influence of the fighting, the embargo, the cuts, and the hysteria that oil historically has produced in otherwise sane people, the price of petroleum skyrocketed. The posted (long-term contract) price immediately went from three dollars to five dollars per barrel, and kept climbing rapidly, while the spot (short-term delivery) price zoomed to twenty

---

[32]Daniel Yergin, *The Prize* (New York, 1991), 567.

dollars. "We weren't bidding just for oil," one harried oil-company executive explained afterward. "We were bidding for our life."[33]

Even those Americans who paid no attention to world politics or international economics quickly felt the impact of the Arab oil embargo. Gasoline prices doubled overnight, then jumped again and again. In many parts of the country, gasoline was frequently unavailable at any price. Suppliers rationed deliveries to dealers, who in turn rationed sales to customers. Service station owners typically turned off the pumps and went home in the middle of the day when they had sold their quotas, forcing drivers to scramble to find other stations still open. Commuters parked their cars overnight in lines leading to gas stations, awaiting the opening of the stations the next morning. In crime-prone neighborhoods, the drivers slept in their cars, sometimes with guns.

The impact of the unprecedented escalation of oil prices was profound and long-lasting. The massive flow of dollars out of the United States drove the final nails into the coffin of the Bretton Woods system. Less than ever was the United States the master of its economic destiny. Inflation climbed to alarming levels in America and most of the rest of the industrialized world. Because energy is a factor of production of nearly every good and service sold in a modern economy, the ballooning of the price of the most important source of energy generated higher prices for nearly everything else. Dislocations caused by the rising cost of energy cut wide swaths through the American economy. The American automobile industry, to name one particularly beleaguered sector of the economy, responded sluggishly to drivers' demands for fuel-stingy cars and commenced a long period of decline relative to Japanese and other foreign carmakers. Worries about inflation contributed to uncertainty about the direction of the American economy, causing an overall slowdown that ratcheted unemployment up. The combination of record inflation and high unemployment evoked a new term, "stagflation," to describe the sad state of the American economy.

Yet for all the damage the petroleum price rises did to the American economy, oil proved a blunt weapon. The Arab embargo was designed to force a change in American policy on the Arab-Israeli issue, but it failed to do so. If anything, the embargo produced a popular backlash in the United States. Few people like being black-

[33]Ibid., 615.

mailed, and Americans in the 1970s liked it no better than anyone else. Some oil executives lobbied for greater sympathy for the Arabs, but at a time of long gasoline lines and unheard-of gas prices, the oil companies were as unpopular as the Arab producers, and the executives' efforts probably did the Arabs more harm than good. Americans were already inclined to look on Israel as the embattled underdog surrounded by enemies. In the most recent case, Israel was the victim of a Pearl Harbor–style sneak attack, and on Yom Kippur, no less. For the most part, the Arab embargo increased the identification of Americans with the Israelis. American ties with Israel, already strong, grew only stronger during the 1970s. As the Arab oil producers recognized the failure of the embargo to cause an American defection from Israel—and, equally important, as they watched non-Arab oil producers such as Iran increase output and seize market share—they decided in the early part of 1974 to drop the embargo.

Washington encouraged this decision by diplomatic efforts toward peace between the Arabs and Israelis. The Nixon administration was singularly unsuited to deal with matters of international economics; high politics—and, in the case of Watergate, low politics—and grand strategy were the forte of Nixon and Kissinger. Economics was for accountants and the business types in the Republican party who paid the party's bills but never warmed to Nixon (not that anyone really did). "Don't talk to me about barrels of oil," Kissinger told aides in the aftermath of the Arab oil embargo. "They might as well be bottles of Coca Cola. I don't understand!"[34]

Yet Kissinger did understand that something had to be done to terminate the quarrel that had produced the embargo. He launched a series of initiatives to bring the Arabs and Israelis to the peace table. These efforts failed to yield the results initially demanded by the embargoing governments; the rights of the Palestinians received nothing more than lip service. But Kissinger's démarche did provide a reasonable pretext for the Saudis, Iraqis, Kuwaitis, Libyans, and so on to get back to the business of selling the Americans oil.

With the Arabs acting more reasonably than before, the Israelis felt required to respond in kind. In their case compromise involved a—slow—softening on territorial questions. The cease-fire that had ended the October War left Israeli and Arab forces locked closely to-

[34]Ibid., 613.

gether, and the next step toward peace required unlocking them. The Israelis and the Egyptians remained within gunshot of each other near the Suez Canal, while the Israelis and Syrians glared and sometimes shouted at each other in the neighborhood of the Golan Heights. Kissinger realized that as long as the opposing armies were at such close quarters, any minor incident might spark another war.

The secretary of state focused first on separating the Israelis and the Egyptians, partly because Egypt was the most important of the Arab countries, and partly because Sadat appeared the most willing of the Arab leaders to make compromises for peace. Progress came grudgingly. The Israelis insisted that their forces retain control of the Mitla and Gidi passes, while the Egyptians demanded that the Israelis give them up. The Egyptians insisted on their right to station a large force on the east bank of the Suez Canal, while the Israelis refused anything more than a token Egyptian unit.

Kissinger found the Israelis especially trying. Though they possessed the strongest military force in the region, they persisted in acting like the underdogs. On one occasion Kissinger became so infuriated with Israeli foreign minister Yigal Allon that he burst out, "For Christ's sake, Yigal—not that that means anything to you . . ." Allon retorted, "Let me remind you, Henry, that Christ was a Jew." They both laughed, easing the tension somewhat. (Nor did less monumental matters facilitate the discussions. Kissinger could hardly abide the food in Israel. "How one million Jewish mothers collectively can cook such awful food is an historical wonder worthy of a good Ph.D. study," he remarked. But he didn't find the food so bad that he wouldn't eat it. Without fail Kissinger gained weight on his negotiating trips. As he explained, when he got nervous he ate; when he negotiated he got nervous. And, he added morosely, he was always negotiating, so he was constantly gaining weight.)[35]

Undaunted by the stubbornness of the two sides, Kissinger shuttled back and forth between Israel and Egypt, and eventually he diminished the distance between their bargaining positions. At the beginning of 1974, he persuaded Egypt to acquiesce in Israeli control of the Sinai passes, and Israel to accept a more-than-token Egyptian contingent on the east bank of the canal. To facilitate the agreement, the Nixon administration promised to support full implementation

[35]Valeriani, *Travels with Henry*, 8; Marvin Kalb and Bernard Kalb, *Kissinger* (Boston, 1974), 527.

of Resolution 242, the 1967 United Nations Security Council measure that somewhat ambiguously called for Israeli withdrawal from the occupied territories in exchange for recognition by the Arabs of Israel's legitimacy. The American promise on Resolution 242 was designed to please Egypt, and it did. To encourage Israel's cooperation, the administration forgave $1 billion in debts the Israelis owed for American weapons.

Kissinger then turned his attention to the northern front in the late war. Disentangling the Israelis and Syrians was harder than disentangling the Israelis and Egyptians. Part of the problem was that Syrian president Hafiz al-Asad lacked the courage and self-confidence of Egypt's Sadat. Another part was that the Israelis were convinced that Syria was abusing prisoners held from the war. Golda Meir told Kissinger, "We will not be present in the same room with the Syrians who are torturing and slaughtering our men! It is elementary!" The greatest part of the problem was that the Golan Heights were strategically vital to the defense of Israel's northeastern border. By contrast to the wide-open spaces of the Sinai, which afforded room for territorial compromise and a margin for military error, the Golan was cramped and unforgiving. Yet even here Kissinger's perseverance paid off. In May 1974, Israel and Syria decided that they had had enough of constant mobilization and agreed to terms of disengagement. An exchange of prisoners accompanied the pact.[36]

Getting from mere disengagement to genuine peace was considerably more difficult. Israel and Egypt were interested, but other important parties weren't. The Syrians demanded the return of the Golan, which the Israelis weren't about to give up. Nor did Asad like the idea of an Egyptian-Israeli peace settlement, because such a settlement would allow the Israelis to turn the full force of their military might against Syria if annoyance again came to war. The Palestinians opposed any settlement that didn't grant them the state they believed was their due. The Soviet Union preferred to keep the Middle Eastern pot boiling as a distraction to the Americans and a potential source of diplomatic influence.

But Egypt and Israel wanted peace with each other more than they wanted to please those who opposed it. Sadat still desired to retrieve the Sinai, and although he continued to support the aspira-

[36]Golan, *Secret Conversations*, 130.

tions of the Palestinians, after a quarter century of efforts on their behalf, including three wars, he judged that the time had come to tend to the needs of his own people. War was expensive, and Egypt was poor. The Israelis similarly were weary from perpetual mobilization. If they could neutralize their largest enemy, they might get at least a little rest.

Kissinger continued to shuttle back and forth between Israel and Egypt through the end of 1974 and into 1975. Much of his time was consumed with pettifogging and posturing by the two parties, but finally, in September 1975, the Egyptians and Israelis signed a second pact. Egypt agreed to resolve its differences with Israel peacefully—a marked shift from its previous insistence that Israel was an illegal entity with no standing in international affairs. Israel agreed to withdraw from the Sinai passes and to give up oil fields in the Sinai it had controlled since 1967.

As before, the United States employed material enticements to nudge each side toward peace. Washington promised the Israelis additional economic and military aid; guaranteed to supply the Israelis the amount of oil they were giving up in the Sinai; pledged prompt consultation in the event the Soviets stepped up their meddling in the region; and vowed not to recognize the Palestine Liberation Organization until the P.L.O. acknowledged Israel's right to exist. Washington promised the Egyptians that it would promote peace talks between Israel and Syria (lest Egypt long be the lone defector from the Arab anti-Israel front); guaranteed Cairo help in constructing a military early-warning system in the Sinai; and committed to consult with Egypt in the event of alleged Israeli violations of the present accord. In addition, the United States would place a team of civilian truce-monitors in the Sinai.

Kissinger initially hoped to keep these American promises to Israel and Egypt secret, but the word soon got out, as any more experienced Middle East hand could have told him it would. (Perhaps Kissinger, one of the most notorious leakers in the modern history of American foreign policy, thought that if he kept his own mouth shut that would suffice.) The news provoked protests both from those persons who thought the United States was giving too much to Egypt and from the smaller number who thought the United States was giving too much to Israel.

The furor did nothing good for the popularity of President Ford, who already bore the onus of having pardoned Richard Nixon. Nor did it do much for Kissinger, whose role in detente had by now infuriated conservatives almost as much as his actions regarding Vietnam had alienated liberals. Under such circumstances, the best Kissinger and Ford could hope for in the Middle East was to defend the gains they had already made toward peace; further gains would have to await a new administration.

By election time in 1976, the odds of America's getting a new administration appeared good. A miracle worker might have led the Republican ticket to victory, but Gerald Ford wasn't a miracle worker.

Like most presidential elections, that of 1976 turned more on domestic affairs than on foreign ones, yet by the mid-1970s the distinction between domestic and foreign affairs was fuzzier than it had been in a long time. Watergate was chiefly a domestic scandal, but one that had been triggered by Nixon's annoyance at criticism of his Vietnam policy and by his desire to silence and politically crush his critics. With good reason, Vietnam and Watergate were often closely linked in the American public mind. Almost as onerous for candidate Ford as Watergate was the unsteady condition of the American economy. Again, this issue was primarily domestic, but it too was significantly affected by international events, notably the collapse of the Bretton Woods system and the leap in world oil prices precipitated by the 1973 Middle East war.

The candidates in the 1976 election could easily have debated such high-profile foreign policy issues as Vietnam and the turmoil in the Middle East (Bretton Woods was rather abstruse for the stump), yet for the most part they didn't. Although Vietnam transformed the way Americans looked at their country's role in the world, the war there was too recent and still too sore a subject for anyone to win political points on. Regarding the Middle East, both political parties stood staunchly behind Israel, and that, essentially, was that. The 1973 Arab attack on Israel and the subsequent Arab oil embargo made standing behind Israel all the easier.

The candidates debated detente somewhat more. Yet even here there was as much agreement as dispute. The conservative counterattack was causing many Republicans to shy away from the policy of warming to the communists. So loud was the criticism and so tenuous Ford's position in the party that the G.O.P. standard-bearer refused to utter the word "detente" in public. At the same time, most

Democrats, while not disliking detente, and content for it to continue, saw no compelling reason to walk point for a policy associated with Richard Nixon and Henry Kissinger.

Behind the absence of really searching debate over foreign policy was the fact that Americans were still trying to sort out what the defeat in Vietnam and the other recent events signified. Vietnam had stunned the American political system, and the shock had yet to wear off. Consequently Americans didn't know how to react to such surprises as Nixon's opening to the communists and the oil-price revolution.

Before much longer, the shock would wear off. When it did, debate would resume, with a vengeance.

CHAPTER 2

False Hopes: 1977–1980

Although Jimmy Carter would have been appalled to be likened to Richard Nixon, in one respect the foreign policies of the two men were similar. Nixon had sought to accommodate America to shifting international circumstances by downgrading anticommunist ideology as the driving force in American foreign affairs. Carter continued the trend.

Yet where Nixon and Henry Kissinger replaced ideology with hard-boiled and even cynical geopolitics, Carter sketched a vision of American foreign relations based on a high-minded idealism Americans hadn't witnessed since Woodrow Wilson. Carter sometimes appeared naive, and events proved that the appearance wasn't always deceiving. But Carter was far from stupid, and he understood that the practice of international relations wasn't the same thing as philanthropy. He simply held that idealism could be a higher form of realism and that America's good name and good example might be worth more than several armored divisions or aircraft carrier groups in ensuring a safe and prosperous future for the United States.

Carter's idealistic approach produced a historic peace agreement between Israel and Egypt, and various lesser accomplishments. But it ultimately fell afoul of some brutal realities of both international affairs and domestic politics. The world continued to grow more unruly, and the status quo inherited from the early postwar period continued to disintegrate. Revolutions in Nicaragua and Iran toppled long-lived regimes, replacing governments friendly to the United States with governments disdainful and sometimes violently hostile. When revolution likewise broke out in Afghanistan, the leadership of the Soviet Union, constrained by no such idealistic notions as Carter's, forcibly suppressed it with the largest military operation mounted by a superpower between the Vietnam War and the Persian Gulf War of 1991.

The revolutionary events abroad afforded ammunition to the opponents of detente in the United States. Initially stymied by the Republican origins of detente, these conservatives delighted in tormenting Carter and the Democratic devotees of the new idealism. Their sniping made Carter's life miserable from the start, but it was only with the overthrow of the pro-American regimes in Managua and Teheran and the Soviet invasion of Afghanistan that they succeeded in stifling the idealism of Carter's foreign policy. Surprisingly, they had help in delivering the coup de grace—from Carter himself.

1. FREE AT LAST?

Carter certainly didn't anticipate ending his presidency as a Cold Warrior. Nor did he guess the degree to which foreign affairs would eventually envelop his administration. The Democratic president recognized that Americans had elected him chiefly for domestic reasons, but like any number of other successful candidates he sought to stretch his mandate as far as it would reach. In his case this involved attempting to recast American foreign relations in a post–Cold War mold. The recasting commenced in an early speech in which he outlined his philosophy of foreign policy. He told his listeners that Americans must understand how much the world had changed in recent years. The ability to control events was slipping out of the hands of the few big countries, including the United States. "We can no longer expect that the other 150 nations will follow the dictates of the powerful," he said. The United States had contributed to the transformation by its tragically misguided policy in Vietnam, which had produced a "profound moral crisis" in America and sapped the faith of other countries in American leadership.

But Vietnam was a symptom rather than the cause of the problem. Americans had been so afraid of communism that they had been willing to support almost any regime that proclaimed itself to be anticommunist. "For too many years," Carter said, "we've been willing to adopt the flawed and erroneous principles and tactics of our adversaries, sometimes abandoning our own values for theirs. We've fought fire with fire, never thinking that fire is better quenched with water." This negative approach had failed, most spectacularly in Vietnam. Yet the debacle in Southeast Asia was not entirely without value, for Americans had learned a lesson from their failure. "We are now free of that inordinate fear of communism which once led us to embrace any dictator who joined us in that fear. I'm glad that that's being changed."

Having denounced the old approach, Carter went on to describe an alternative. He advocated genuinely serious efforts to halt the arms race. "This race is not only dangerous, it's morally deplorable," he declared. "We must put an end to it." He called for efforts to remedy world poverty. "More than 100 years ago, Abraham Lincoln said that our country could not exist half slave and half free. We know a peaceful world cannot long exist one-third rich and two-thirds hungry."

Most strikingly, Carter stressed the need to insist on justice in every government's treatment of its citizens. He stated that a commitment to human rights must be a centerpiece of American policy. Some persons, he said, argued that security had to come first and that human rights were a dispensable luxury. He couldn't disagree more. "The great democracies are not free because we are strong and prosperous," he asserted. "We are strong and influential and prosperous because we are free." The only appropriate basis for American policy was the moral foundation on which the American republic had been established. "Our policy is rooted in our moral values. Our policy is designed to serve mankind."[1]

Though conservatives hooted and whistled at Carter's dreaminess, Congress and the American public initially supported the president's vision. After the cynicism that had produced Vietnam and Watergate, a dose of idealism seemed like just what the doctor ordered. Occasionally Americans enjoy being encouraged to live up to their angels rather than down to their devils; everyone does. Moreover, Carter's idealistic approach was morally fortifying in that it told Americans that here was someone—and not just *some*one but their chosen leader—who believed that there was a place in the world for moral values. After thirty years of Cold War realpolitik, this was quite a breath of fresh air.

Swept up in the idealism of the hour, Congress passed a resolution proclaiming that the promotion of human rights should be a primary goal of the United States. The legislature also directed the president to certify that foreign governments receiving American

[1]*Public Papers of the Presidents: Carter,* May 22, 1977.

aid were respecting the rights of their citizens, or at least making progress toward that goal. Violators would be booted off the aid rolls.

Carter went beyond the congressional directive on human rights. He created a special State Department office for human rights and named as director Patricia Derian, a battle-hardened civil rights advocate from Mississippi. Derian delighted in mixing it up with conservatives who contended that the United States needed to cultivate governments that were pro-American even if moderately repressive. "What the hell is moderately repressive?" she demanded. "That you only torture half of the people? That you only do summary executions now and then?"[2]

Carter didn't leave human rights to Derian. The president carried on a highly public correspondence with Soviet dissident Andrei Sakharov, much to the Kremlin's displeasure. He actively promoted United Nations resolutions on human rights, calling them "tangible steps toward the realization of both peace among nations and the preservation of human rights for individual men and women throughout the world." He enforced trade sanctions against the whites-only Ian Smith government of Rhodesia (soon Zimbabwe) and against the tyrannical Idi Amin government of Uganda.[3]

In keeping with the congressional resolution, the president slashed American aid to the repressive governments of Anastasio Somoza of Nicaragua and Augusto Pinochet of Chile, and he applied similar pressure against a violently rightist military junta in Argentina. He embargoed weapons and police equipment to the apartheid regime of South Africa. He warned the rulers of Iran, the Philippines, and South Korea that they might expect sanctions if they didn't stop abusing their citizens.

Simultaneously with his human rights offensive, Carter pushed forward on the arms control front. He declared his desire to go beyond the SALT I accords of the 1972 Nixon-Brezhnev summit and a subsequent interim pact initialed by Ford and Brezhnev at Vladivostok in 1974, toward the goal of seriously slowing the buildup of superpower weaponry. He ordered his principal negotiators, Paul Warnke and Secretary of State Cyrus Vance, to keep at their Soviet counterparts until the latter agreed to lower the caps on strategic weapons.

[2]Donald S. Spencer, *The Carter Implosion* (New York, 1988), 57–58.
[3]*Public Papers*, Oct. 5, 1977.

The Soviets registered deep skepticism, chiefly because they didn't know what to think of an administration that placed such emphasis on idealism and morality in foreign affairs. Were the Americans really serious about this? If so, should we hold out for a better deal?

Eventually the Soviets decided that whether or not the Americans were serious about their idealism, arms control made sense from the perspective of Soviet interests. After two years of exhortation and negotiation, Carter got Brezhnev's signature on a 1979 SALT II treaty that reduced the number of launchers allowed to each side (from 2,400 to 2,250) and placed limits on other parts of the superpower arsenals.

Carter also elevated the visibility of the poor and non-industrialized countries in American foreign relations. Calling for a shift in emphasis from the East-West issues that had dominated the Cold War to so-called North-South issues of equity in the distribution of the planet's resources, he hired several individuals for whom the latter issues were a priority. The most visible and audible of these individuals was Andrew Young, Carter's ambassador to the United Nations. Young was the first African-American to hold that post, and he took pains to consult with the representatives of the African, Asian, and Latin American countries that constituted a majority of the U.N. General Assembly. (Young took fewer pains to consult with others in the Carter administration. His boss at the State Department, Cyrus Vance, grew increasingly annoyed at what he judged Young's freelancing. Three months into Carter's term, National Security Adviser Zbigniew Brzezinski wrote of Vance: "I have not seen him so put off for quite a long time, and I think it's obvious that Andy is beginning to get under his skin.")[4]

Like Carter, Young rejected the idea commonly in evidence in American policy during the Cold War that American security required collaborating with rightist dictators against leftist revolutionaries. Young held that such an approach was counterproductive: that by collaborating with the reactionaries Washington drove the revolutionaries even farther to the left and often into the arms of Moscow.

Young also urged a more equal allocation of the world's wealth. The hope of a better life, he contended, was the best defense

[4]Zbigniew Brzezinski, *Power and Principle* (New York, 1985 ed.), 37.

against communism. And poverty was as dangerous a foe of human rights as the most tyrannical dictatorship. "These rights are hollow for any individual who starves to death," Young said. The United States must accommodate itself to change. "We need not fear change if we build into it more equity and more participation. Indeed, fear of social change is the thing we need to fear the most. If we are afraid of it and try to preserve that which is eroding beneath our feet, we will fail." Americans must recognize how thoroughly the world was changing. "I believe that we are at the end of the period of cold wars, in the middle of the era of detente, and just beginning to find ways to build the structures of cooperation." Cooperation wouldn't always come easily to a world used to confrontation. But neither was it impossible. "I believe that cooperation for the common good of humankind can be as powerful an incentive to our imagination as fear for our survival."[5]

Neither Carter's campaign for human rights nor his efforts on behalf of the planet's poor produced anything as measurably concrete as the SALT II treaty (which, counting missile silos as it did, was about as measurably concrete as you could get). Carter's initiatives helped spring some high-visibility dissidents from foreign jails—Benigno Aquino of the Philippines and Jacobo Timerman of Argentina being prime examples—but the nature of repression is such that most occurs beyond the view of the world, and this went on about as before (although the American attention may have changed its form somewhat: the military ruler of Brazil was reported as saying, "I intend to open this country up to democracy. And anyone who is against that, I will jail, I will crush!"). Andrew Young's declarations on behalf of the impoverished and oppressed may have sensitized people in the United States and elsewhere to the concerns of the Third World, but global poverty and inequality had taken millennia to develop and weren't going to be erased in the space of one presidential term.[6]

2. PERSISTENCE PAYS

In one area, however, Carter's efforts paid substantial dividends. Though Henry Kissinger's reservoir of influence on Middle Eastern

[5]*American Foreign Policy: Basic Documents 1977–1980* (Washington, 1983), 432–34.
[6]Spencer, *Carter Implosion*, 60.

issues had run dry by 1976, the governments of Egypt and Israel remained interested in normalizing relations between their countries. Egypt's Sadat more than ever wanted to get back the Sinai and get on to business besides the quarrel with Israel, and he was prepared to risk the wrath of his many critics in the Arab world. Israel's Menachem Begin, prime minister as of June 1977, wanted a peace treaty with the foremost of the Arab states. Like many other Israeli hardliners, Begin insisted that the West Bank rightfully belonged to Israel and must not be relinquished, but he had no such attachment to the Sinai. The cantankerous Begin might be difficult to deal with in negotiations, but any concessions he did make would probably be acceptable to the Israeli parliament, or Knesset, on the same kind of reasoning that had caused the American Congress to accept Richard Nixon's opening to China.

Jimmy Carter provided the catalyst necessary for peace between the Egyptians and the Israelis. More than any other president before or since, Carter took a personal interest in the Arab-Israeli dispute. To some extent, his interest reflected his deeply held Christian beliefs. Whenever Carter picked up his Bible, which he did daily, he was reminded of the Holy Land. Carter deemed it a worthy goal to help bring peace to the places where Jesus had walked. In addition, Carter was deeply impressed by Sadat. "On April 4, 1977," he wrote, "a shining light burst on the Middle East scene for me. I had my first meeting with President Anwar Sadat of Egypt, a man who would change history and whom I would come to admire more than any other leader."[7]

Carter was considerably less taken by Menachem Begin. Recalling an appearance of the Israeli prime minister on an American television interview program, Carter noted in his diary, "It was frightening to watch his adamant position on issues that must be resolved if a Middle Eastern peace settlement is going to be realized."[8]

Carter received scant encouragement from the American political establishment in his effort to bring peace to the Middle East. As a newcomer to Washington, the president summoned the so-called Wise Men of Democratic politics—former high officials with long experience in government—to sound them out on the prospects for an American-sponsored peace initiative. They warned him to keep his distance. The Arab-Israeli dispute was so intractable as to im-

[7]Jimmy Carter, *Keeping Faith* (Toronto, 1982), 282.
[8]Ibid., 288.

peril any president who ventured near. He should concentrate on easier problems.

But Carter chose to try anyway. After much ground-clearing, he invited Sadat and Begin to join him at Camp David, the presidential hideaway in the Maryland mountains. The meeting was originally scheduled to last three days but stretched to nearly two weeks. The start of the meeting was hardly auspicious. Sadat presented an opening position so uncompromising as to threaten to kill the conference on the spot. "As I read it my heart sank," Carter wrote. "It was extremely harsh and filled with all the unacceptable Arab rhetoric." Begin's opening position wasn't much more promising, and before long the Israeli delegation was packing its bags and making as if to go home.[9]

Carter saved the day by dropping his original idea of face-to-face meetings between Begin and Sadat in favor of meetings between himself and the two leaders individually. Sadat helped matters by telling Carter that Egypt's tough opening stance was merely a bargaining position. If Carter would suggest compromises, Egypt might be able to accept them.

Carter had less rapport with Begin than with Sadat. But here Zbigniew Brzezinski came in handy. Like the Israeli prime minister, Carter's national security adviser was a native of Poland; like Begin (and unlike Carter at this stage), Brzezinski believed in the efficacy of force to resolve otherwise unyielding international problems; like Begin (and again unlike Carter at this time), he was deeply suspicious of anything relating to the Soviet Union. And like Begin, Brzezinski enjoyed a vigorous game of chess. The two would play after a hard day's negotiating. Over their initial game Begin announced that this was the first time he had played since 1940, when in the middle of another game the Soviet secret police had burst in and carried him off to prison. After Begin blindsided him and captured his queen, Brzezinski doubted the tale. His doubts intensified when Begin's wife entered the room and said, "Menachem just loves to play chess!"[10]

Whether from Brzezinski's influence or for his own reasons, Begin showed greater flexibility in private sessions than in his public

[9]Ibid., 340.
[10]Brzezinski, *Power and Principle*, 259.

statements. Slowly Carter managed to diminish the distance between the Israelis and the Egyptians.

Recognizing that the Sinai held the key to a settlement between Egypt and Israel, Carter separated that subject conceptually from the others that vexed Arab-Israeli relations. The West Bank, the Gaza Strip, the Golan Heights, the future of the Palestinians: these harder items were left for later. Sadat and Begin should focus on the Sinai.

Yet even an agreement on the Sinai didn't come readily. Though the Sinai meant less to most Israelis than, for example, the West Bank (which hard-liners like Begin considered part of historical Israel and called by the biblical names of Judea and Samaria), it meant a lot to the residents of the housing settlements the Israelis had established there since the 1967 war. Begin initially insisted that Israel could not remove the settlements, as Egypt was demanding. "We don't dismantle settlements," he said adamantly. "We don't plow them up or demolish them." At another moment the Israeli prime minister indicated even greater determination. "My right eye will fall out," he

The smiles disguise the difficulty Jimmy Carter has had in bringing Menachem Begin and Anwar el-Sadat to an agreement. Carter keeps a grip on Begin, who has been threatening to walk out of the Camp David talks. *Carter Library.*

told Brzezinski, "my right hand will fall off before I ever agree to the dismantling of a single Jewish settlement."[11]

Eventually, however, Begin softened his opposition. He said he would leave the matter to the Knesset to decide. Sadat accepted this arrangement on the condition that if the Israeli parliament refused to remove the settlements, Egypt would be released from its part of any bargain.

On the thirteenth day, as everyone involved was about to collapse of exhaustion, Carter guided the hands of Sadat and Begin to the signing of an accord. The heart of the Camp David agreement was a promise by Egypt to extend diplomatic recognition to Israel in exchange for Israel's withdrawal from the Sinai and the removal of the settlements. The two sides additionally agreed to conclude a peace treaty. Issues of primary importance to the Palestinians and other Arabs were left in diplomatic limbo, shrouded in language that the opposing parties could interpret to their own benefit and that committed no one to anything inconvenient.

Between September 1978 and the early part of 1979, representatives of Israel and Egypt, with continuing nudges from the U.S. government, worked out the details of the promised peace treaty. On March 26, 1979, Sadat again met Begin, this time in Washington, to sign the treaty. As in the earlier Egyptian-Israeli agreements, the United States provided tasty morsels that made the pact more palatable to both sides. The Carter administration promised the Israelis $3 billion in new aid and confirmed its prior guarantee of a supply of oil to Israel. The administration pledged $1.5 billion in aid to Egypt. These commitments soon made Israel and Egypt the largest recipients of American foreign aid, a status they retained through the mid-1990s. Occasionally members of Congress would grumble at all the money going to just two countries, but for the most part the legislators granted that if the money bought peace between the Arabs and Israel, it was money well spent.

3. SANDINO LIVES!

The Camp David accord and the consequent peace treaty between Egypt and Israel were the most significant accomplishments of the

---

[11]Ezer Weizmann, *The Battle for Peace* (New York, 1981), 364; Brzezinski, *Power and Principle*, 263.

Carter administration, demonstrating the president's determination, his powers of persuasion, and his mastery of detail. Another diplomatic achievement of the Carter administration reflected similar qualities. But where nearly everyone in the United States applauded Carter's actions in helping write the Israeli-Egyptian treaty, many roundly criticized his role in rewriting the treaties governing U.S. relations with Panama.

The Panama treaties were a legacy of the bumptious days of Theodore Roosevelt, when the United States had assisted Panama to win independence from Colombia and had received in return the right to build a canal across the country and to control a zone ten miles wide surrounding the canal. The loss of sovereignty over such a comparatively large part of their small country had long rankled Panamanians, and in 1964 they staged violent riots to express their displeasure. Lyndon Johnson consented to revise the treaties, but the process dragged on for more than a decade afterward. Carter, in keeping with his professed sensitivity to the concerns of the less powerful, determined to drive the revision process to a conclusion. He succeeded relatively quickly, and in September 1977 his administration agreed to two treaties with Panama, one restoring sovereignty over the canal zone to Panama by the year 2000, the other pledging the perpetual neutrality of the canal.

Not many people outside Panama had been paying attention to the treaty negotiations, but when word got out that the Carter administration intended for the United States to relinquish control of the canal, the proposed treaties triggered a political lightning storm. Some of the thunderbolts were thrown sincerely, their hurlers wondering why the United States ought to hand over control of the vital waterway to a small country with a history of unrest. Others were thrown for partisan reasons, by Republicans using the canal treaties to try to score points against the Democrats. Still others were more ideological, designed to cast doubt on Carter's judgment and thereby discredit detente.

All three kinds of opposition took a toll, and the president had to give his best effort to garner the votes necessary for the Senate to approve the treaties. Treaty advocates pointed out that the canal was subject to sabotage, as it traversed miles of dense jungle and included several locks. They contended that the canal would be safer in the hands of satisfied Panamanians than in the hands of an American military that had to defend it against angry Panamanians. They also noted that the canal wasn't as vital as it once had been, what with the development of oversized cargo ships that couldn't fit through the locks and with improvements in rail and highway transport across North America.

Carter's critics didn't block the treaties, but they did force the administration to attach a statement reserving to the United States the right to defend the neutrality of the canal after Panama assumed control. The precise wording of the attachment occasioned some sparring with the Panamanian government and prolonged the debate in the United States. Ultimately, however, the Senate approved the two treaties, sixty-eight to thirty-two. Had two senators changed their votes, the treaties would have lacked the necessary two-thirds majority and gone down to defeat. Carter correctly claimed a victory, but it was a victory that left him wounded.

This was bad news for the administration, for Carter needed all his strength when an even sharper controversy developed over events elsewhere in Central America. For decades, the political situation in Nicaragua had been in a state of turmoil. American troops had occupied that country off and on from the first part of the century through the 1930s, when the rebel leader Augusto Sandino had been killed by elements of the Nicaraguan National Guard, headed by Anastasio Somoza. Somoza ruled until the mid-1950s, when he was assassinated. He was succeeded by two sons, Luis and Anastasio, who carried on the family tradition of monopolizing power through political corruption, firm control of the police and military, and careful cultivation of the United States, which contributed economic and military aid.

The Somozas' rule provoked opposition, led by members of the educated class who objected to the family's hogging all the good opportunities for getting ahead. The younger Anastasio, who gradually took charge, judged it prudent to let some of the dissidents air their grievances in newspapers, not least since the editor of the leading opposition paper, Pedro Chamorro, had connections among people Anastasio didn't desire to alienate completely. Besides, most of the ordinary people in Nicaragua couldn't read, and consequently Somoza didn't worry much about what the papers carried. By contrast, he kept a tight lid on radio and television.

During the early 1970s, leadership of the opposition began to shift to the radical Sandinista National Liberation Front (F.S.L.N.). At first the Sandinistas confined most of their activities to guerrilla raids from bases in the mountains, annoying but not seriously threatening the Somoza regime. A turning point, however, came in 1972 when a devastating earthquake flattened Managua and momentarily focused the attention of the world on Nicaragua. Dozens of foreign countries sent emergency aid, much of which Somoza and his cronies siphoned off into their private bank accounts. For many Nicaraguans, this outrage was the last straw, and the Sandinistas soon gained the reputation of Robin Hoods. At the end of 1974 a group of F.S.L.N. commandos raided a Christmas party in the capital and seized several hostages, whom they held until they received a large ransom and the release of a number of F.S.L.N. members held in Somoza's jails.

Somoza responded with a major antiguerrilla offensive. Assisted by American military aid, his soldiers chased the Sandinistas around the countryside and harassed, sometimes killed, persons suspected of supporting the rebels. At the time Carter entered the White House in January 1977 the violence in Nicaragua had become a full-scale civil war, replete with the atrocities civil wars frequently produce.

Carter found himself pulled two ways on Nicaragua. On one hand, he wished to distance the United States from the brutal aspects of Somoza's regime. On the other, he didn't desire to destabilize Nicaragua and deliver it to radicals who openly expressed their enmity toward the United States.

Carter's ambivalence reflected disputes within his administration. Secretary of State Vance and other advocates of human rights wanted the president to use American aid as a lever to force reforms on Somoza. Brzezinski and other hawks feared that forcing reforms on Somoza would weaken the Nicaraguan government and open the floodgates to radical revolution. The dispute began as a philosophical difference but became personal. Vance and the State Department grew convinced that Brzezinski and the National Security Council staff were connivers who delighted in disrupting official American policy; Brzezinski and company believed that the diplomats were hopeless softheads and irredeemable paper-pushers. (It was a measure of the bitterness of the dispute that Patricia Derian, reviewing Brzezinski's memoirs for the *Washington Post*, called it the story of how Brzezinski "tried to cut the throats of everyone who stood in the path of his power and strategic principle"—and that Brzezinski considered this such a sufficient commendation that he had it printed on the back cover of the book's paperback edition.)

Zbigniew Brzezinski and Cyrus Vance. Notice
that they are both talking at the same time.
Carter Library.

Carter tolerated the squabbling between Vance and Brzezinski as
the price of sound advice. As in other areas, Carter deliberately distanced himself from the Nixon administration; the Democratic president thought that much of what had gone wrong under Nixon was the
result of Kissinger's monopoly of access to the Oval Office. Condoning
the backbiting between Brzezinski and Vance was Carter's way of ensuring that no one cornered the market on access in *his* administration.
"I needed to weigh as many points of view as possible," the president
explained. Besides, for all his respect for Vance as an administrator and
negotiator, Carter, like others, found him a bit boring. Brzezinski, by
contrast, brought excitement to the administration. "Next to members
of my family, Zbig would be my favorite seatmate on a long-distance
trip; we might argue, but I would never be bored."[12]

In the case of Nicaragua, Carter sought a middle ground between Vance and Brzezinski. In an effort to improve the Nicaraguan

[12]Carter, *Keeping Faith*, 54.

status quo without handing the country to the leftists, the president warned Somoza to shape up. He criticized Nicaragua's human rights record and told Somoza to broaden participation in his government if he wanted to return to the good graces of the United States. Carter didn't pull the plug on American aid entirely, but he did cut back on military assistance.

Somoza didn't take the American suggestions well, instead digging in his heels. In January 1978 some of Somoza's thugs murdered Pedro Chamorro. The assassination of the most visible moderate opponent of the government caused revulsion worldwide and strengthened the hand of the radicals in Nicaragua. Many surviving moderates hoped that the United States would now see the light and push Somoza out of power. But Carter, beset by conservative criticism of his handling of the Panama treaties and reluctant to intervene directly in Nicaragua's affairs, declined to take such strong action.

Carter's diffidence contributed to a leftward shift of the Nicaraguan revolution, as the moderates decided that the only way they could get rid of Somoza was to make common cause with the radicals. During the summer of 1978, Sandinista commandos accomplished their most spectacular feat to date: the capture of the National Palace and the capture there of more than one thousand hostages. Before releasing the hostages and evacuating the palace, the commandos won the freedom of scores of prisoners and safe passage out of the country to Panama. (Although by this time the U.S. Senate had approved the Panama treaties, the fact that the Panamanian government accepted the Nicaraguan rebels allowed American conservatives to criticize Carter's policies toward both Nicaragua and Panama in a single breath.)

Somoza held on for several more months, during which the violence and disorder in Nicaragua escalated. The Carter administration continued to try to find a middle ground between the dictator and the radical Sandinistas. Carter again expostulated with Somoza to change his ways and give moderate reformers a voice in running the country. But he couldn't bring himself to cut Somoza off entirely, and the Nicaraguan strongman ignored most of Washington's remonstrances. Force had worked for the Somozas in the past, and this Somoza believed it would work again.

Only when the situation became hopeless for Somoza did Carter change his policy. In June 1979, administration representatives joined officials of the Organization of American States in calling for a cease-fire agreement that included Somoza's resignation. Yet events were moving faster than U.S. policy, and the Sandinistas insisted on total victory.

It arrived the next month when Somoza fled Managua for Miami, where he became a headache for the Carter administration by apparently plotting a return to power. Carter's conservative critics didn't object to such a scheme, but the administration by now was trying to establish a basis for understanding with the successor government in Nicaragua, and it simply wanted Somoza to go away. He eventually did, to Paraguay, that traditional haven for ex-Nazis and other rightists on the run. Paraguay didn't prove such a haven for Somoza: he was murdered there in 1980, evidently by Argentine assassins who had their own reasons for wishing him dead.

The departure of Somoza solved some of Carter's problems with respect to Nicaragua but created others. Carter self-consciously tried to avoid what he considered to be the mistakes of the Eisenhower administration in dealing with the Cuban revolution twenty years earlier. At that time Washington had waged political and economic warfare against the new Castro regime, thereby virtually guaranteeing that Cuba would turn to the Soviet Union for help. Carter went out of his way not to apply pressure against the Sandinista-led government in Nicaragua, and he even asked Congress for $75 million in economic aid to help rebuild the country after the civil war.

Yet while Carter tried to be nice to the new government in Nicaragua, his critics demanded that he take a tougher line. Seizing on the anti-Yankee rhetoric and Marxist-Leninist leanings of some of the Sandinistas, and on the presence of numerous advisers from Cuba, the conservatives opposed aid to the Sandinistas. The administration finally prevailed on Congress in July 1980 to approve the assistance, but the long delay and the acerbic debate the bill provoked drastically diminished whatever good will it might have produced toward the United States in Nicaragua. Carter was left in the unenviable position of having alienated both American conservatives, by helping a government that was seen as dangerously radical, and the Nicaraguan government, by providing aid too grudgingly and too late.

4. THE SHAH AND THE AYATOLLAH

If the outcome of events in Nicaragua was a disappointment to the Carter administration, the outcome of events in Iran was a disaster. The ruler of Iran at the time of Carter's 1977 inauguration had been in power even longer than Nicaragua's Somoza, and like the Nicaraguan leader, the shah of Iran owed much of his official longevity to American assistance. The shah, Muhammad Reza Pahlavi, had ascended the Peacock Throne in 1941, but until the early 1950s he reigned more than he ruled. A 1953 coup engineered by the C.I.A. with the assistance of Britain's spy service changed the situation by overthrowing the leading political figure of the day, the insufficiently anticommunist Prime Minister Muhammad Mussadiq, and delivering power to the shah. Without publicly owning up to the American role in the coup, Washington endorsed its result by shipping several hundred million dollars in economic and military aid to the shah during the next few years. And it said little as the shah instituted measures to suppress dissent, although those measures included provisions that blatantly trampled the civil liberties of many Iranians.

Under John Kennedy, the United States made marginally greater efforts to get the shah to moderate his harsher measures. Partly to placate Washington, and partly from his own judgment of what was necessary and appropriate, the shah ordered a modest land-redistribution program, various educational improvements, and curbs on corruption. Though the reforms got Washington off his back—and kept American aid flowing—they did little to ameliorate the plight of Iran's poor. At the same time, the shah's policies generated hostility both among members of the urban middle class, who wanted the government to move more rapidly in modernizing Iran, and among Shiite Muslim fundamentalists, who wanted the government to move more slowly—or, preferably, to reverse course.

The hostility to the shah intensified during the late 1960s and early 1970s, and American actions did little to mitigate it. The Nixon administration nominated Iran to be a pro-Western policeman in the Persian Gulf region, and to this end Nixon showered upon the shah all the weapons the Iranian monarch's money could buy. Direct American aid played a smaller role in Iran's finances than before, but the shah didn't need the aid after the big jump in oil prices in the early 1970s started pouring money into the royal coffers almost faster than he could figure out how to spend it. The Arab oil embargo of 1973 also worked in Iran's favor by allowing Iran to seize a larger share of the world oil market.

Tactlessly and arrogantly—but such are often the traits of unearned wealth and power—the shah lectured the West on the "noble" character of petroleum and on the need for people in countries such as the United States to recognize that the era of cheap energy had ended. "They will have to tighten their belts; eventually all those children of well-to-do families who have plenty to eat at every meal, who have their cars . . . they will have to rethink all these aspects of the advanced industrial world." When the shah, one of the richest men on the planet due to sheer geological good luck, went on to say that Americans and other Westerners must get out and "earn their living," he lost even more friends.[13]

Beyond Nixon's strategic purpose of bolstering the shah as an agent of a pro-Western status quo in the Persian Gulf, the American policy of massive arms sales to Iran had two additional objectives: recycling Iran's petrodollars to alleviate the balance-of-payments problems the big rise in oil prices was causing the United States, and maintaining the profitability of American weapons manufacturers in the post-Vietnam era, when the American Defense Department was cutting back on arms purchases. From this combination of reasons, sales of American weapons to Iran reached record levels during the mid-1970s. The chief of the American military advisory group in Teheran recalled the period as "a salesman's dream."[14]

Unfortunately for fruitful U.S.-Iranian relations, the billions spent on American weapons fostered an impression in many Iranians that the shah cared more about flashy military hardware than about the welfare of the Iranian people. With so many poor in Iran, couldn't the shah find better uses for the country's money than planes and tanks and guns? That the weapons came with American advisers, technicians, and other support personnel reminded Iranians of the large role the United States had played and continued to play in the shah's exercise of power. Moreover, the presence of the more than twenty thousand Americans, nearly all of whom were non-Muslim, was interpreted as an affront and a threat by the Is-

[13]Daniel Yergin, *The Prize* (New York, 1991), 626.
[14]Barry Rubin, *Paved with Good Intentions* (New York, 1980), 135.

lamic fundamentalists who already objected to the shah's Westernizing policies.

By 1977, Iran was about to explode, and Jimmy Carter had to decide whether to try to prevent the explosion or simply get out of the way of the shrapnel. The president received conflicting advice, just as he did regarding Nicaragua, and from the same two camps within his administration. Vance and many of the career diplomats advocated pressure on the shah to shape up. Unless the shah did so, these liberals argued, he would deliver Iran into the hands of individuals, such as the radical Islamic fundamentalists, who felt nothing but hatred for the United States. For the administration to act as though nothing were happening, and to continue to express confidence in the shah's handling of Iranian affairs, would cause him to resist reforms of any sort, thereby discrediting moderates in Iran and strengthening the hand of the Islamic radicals.

Brzezinski and the self-styled realists in the administration, on the other hand, advocated solid support for the shah. Viewing Iran chiefly in the context of relations with the Soviet Union, the Brzezinski group reminded Carter that keeping the Soviets away from the Persian Gulf had been an American priority since World War II. Although the shah fell somewhat short of the human rights standards of Amnesty International, he had been a faithful American ally for twenty-five years and remained firmly opposed to the extension of Soviet influence. The radicals who were working for the shah's removal might not be communists themselves, but they could easily prove so weak and disorganized as to lay themselves open to Moscow's intimidation. Besides, there was the larger issue of American credibility. In the aftermath of Vietnam, governments all over the world were watching to see whether Washington would honor its commitments or cut and run when things got difficult. If the United States backed out on the shah, American credibility would vanish. Better to stand by the shah, even in a losing battle, than to surrender.

Carter had as hard a time making up his mind on Iran as he had on Nicaragua. At first the president allied himself with Vance and the doves. He warned the shah that unless the Iranian government loosened restrictions on dissent it would suffer Washington's displeasure. The president sent Vance to Teheran in early 1977 to underline the significance Washington placed on human rights. "I stressed their importance as a key element of our foreign policy,"

Vance said later. "I emphasized that the president was committed to reaffirming the primacy of human rights as a national goal."

But the shah chose not to hear. "He said that his regime was under attack from within by Communists and assorted fellow travelers," Vance reported, "and that there were limits on how far he could go in restraining his security forces. He warned that if Iran were to slip into civil strife, only the Soviet Union would stand to gain."[15]

As Nicaragua's Somoza was doing at the same time, the shah was sizing up the Carter administration and concluding that Washington wouldn't abandon him. As long as he could make a reasonable argument that he alone kept Iran from radical instability, the American government would continue to support him. In this respect, he had little incentive to reform and much incentive to crack down harder than ever, precisely to polarize the situation in Iran. The Americans might prefer moderates to himself, but they would never side with radicals against him.

Despite Carter's warning, the American government didn't give much indication of seriousness about reform in Iran. After Vance's speech on the importance of human rights, the secretary of state told the shah that the administration had just approved Iran's request to purchase 160 high-performance F-16 aircraft. In addition, the administration was planning to lobby Congress in favor of approval for the delivery of several flying radar stations (AWACs). The shah expressed satisfaction at the news, and without missing a beat asked for 140 additional F-16s.

Carter continued to pay lip service to human rights in Iran, but refused to make the matter a priority. To some extent, he was deterred by the shah's refusal to budge. To some extent, he was responding to Brzezinski's whispering in his ear about American credibility. Bolstering Brzezinski's argument was the barrage of criticism Carter was suffering from the American right. Already under fire for his handling of the Nicaraguan situation, and needing every vote he could muster for the Panama Canal treaties, Carter couldn't afford more enemies.

The shah had an additional trump card beyond the threat of laying Iran open to the radicals. Though Iran had been the pushiest of the OPEC members pushing for higher prices during the early 1970s, by the latter part of the decade he was showing signs that he

---

[15]Cyrus Vance, *Hard Choices* (New York, 1983), 318–19.

might take a softer line. Skeptics ascribed this to no love for the United States but rather to concern that the oil-fired inflation afflicting America was eroding the value of his dollar-denominated investments, and that high prices, which had already driven the consuming countries to conservation, might permanently weaken the market for oil. Whatever the reason, Washington hoped that gentle handling of the shah would encourage him toward cooperation on prices.

Carter definitely handled the shah gently when the president brought him to Washington in the autumn of 1977. Carter breathed hardly a word about human rights in Iran, instead relating happily that Congress had approved the administration's request for the AWACs for Iran. When the shah said that his latest analysis indicated that the 140 extra F-16s wouldn't suffice, and that he needed 70 beyond those, Carter obligingly answered that he would see what he could do about providing them. For his part, the shah promised to try to hold the line on oil prices at the upcoming December meeting of OPEC.

Jimmy Carter listens to the shah of Iran confidently explain how he will handle the Iranian opposition.
Carter Library.

The shah's visit provoked violent demonstrations by large numbers of Iranians in the United States. One such demonstration just outside the White House grounds attracted thousands of people and led to fighting between pro-shah demonstrators and a larger number of anti-shah demonstrators. Washington police tried to break up the crowd with tear gas, some of which wafted over the fence to the White House lawn, where Carter, the shah, and assorted other dignitaries were lavishing compliments on one another. The incident produced red eyes among the Carter-shah contingent and red faces at police headquarters. It also caused Carter to reflect, after the fact, on the meaning of it all. "That day—November 15, 1977—was an augury," Carter wrote. "The tear gas had created the semblance of grief. Almost two years later, and for fourteen months afterward, there would be real grief in our country because of Iran."[16]

The shah wasn't crying, however, as he departed for home. "The shah left Washington encouraged by his conversations with the president," Vance recalled, "and we received from the embassy in Tehran glowing reports of a new mood of confidence and satisfaction."[17]

That the shah could feel this way indicated how far out of touch with events he had become. Ever since a 1971 extravaganza celebrating twenty-five hundred years of the Persian monarchy, at which the shah likened himself to Cyrus the Great and other legendary Persian heroes, many observers had noted a growing megalomania in him, and an increasing disconnectedness from the lives of ordinary Iranians. "Do you really have to bribe people?" he asked a German interviewer who informed him of the corruption that pervaded daily contacts with government officials.[18]

Compounding the trouble was the fact that the shah was dying of cancer and knew it. His declining condition depressed him and clouded his judgment. As a result he was increasingly unable to get a grip on the course of developments in Iran.

The shah wasn't entirely unaware of the need for change, though. He instituted a few modest reforms: amnesty for some political prisoners, an easing of press restraints, a relaxation of laws against political opposition. But as time passed, the demands for change from the shah's growing numbers of critics only intensified,

[16]Carter, *Keeping Faith*, 434.
[17]Vance, *Hard Choices*, 321–23.
[18]Rubin, *Paved with Good Intentions*, 212.

and his reforms often appeared to indicate weakness rather than magnanimity.

Carter traveled to Iran at the end of 1977. While there, the president praised the shah's "great leadership" and the "respect and the admiration and love" with which the Iranian people viewed their monarch. Carter described Iran as "an island of stability in one of the most troubled areas of the world."[19]

But the island hid a volcano. The president had hardly left Iran when the country erupted. On January 9, 1978, an event took place that was to the Iranian revolution what the storming of the Bastille was to the French revolution, and the battles of Lexington and Concord were to the American revolution. On that day a crowd of theology students in the sacred city of Qom protested an article by the shah's information minister criticizing the exiled ayatollah Ruhollah Khomeini. Police fired on the students, killing some two dozen and wounding many more.

The killings triggered a wave of outrage that spread across the country. In February, rioting broke out in Tabriz, a city with special significance in the history of Iranian nationalism. Within weeks the violence spread to Teheran, where the authorities sent tanks into the streets against the demonstrators. After the government blocked further demonstrations, the religious opposition called a general strike. At the end of May, violence shook the campus of Teheran University. In July, the city of Meshed burst into anti-shah anarchy. In August, the worst fighting in Iran thus far hit Isfahan. At the beginning of September, after the imposition of martial law in Teheran, a huge crowd gathered in the capital's Jaleh Square. Army officers ordered the crowd to disperse, and when it didn't the soldiers opened fire. Hundreds were killed and thousands wounded. Running gunfights rattled the city for the rest of the day.

The Jaleh Square incident occurred while Jimmy Carter was ensconced at Camp David with Sadat and Begin. The president placed a phone call to Teheran to assure the shah of America's support. Shortly thereafter the White House issued a statement confirming the close relationship between the United States and Iran, regretting the loss of life in Teheran, and hoping the violence would end and Iran's evolution toward democracy would continue.

Although this statement indicated that Washington still stood

[19] *American Foreign Policy*, 723–24.

by the shah, doubts within the administration about the wisdom of such a policy were increasing. Early in November the American ambassador to Iran, William Sullivan, sent a long telegram to the State Department analyzing the situation. Entitled "Thinking the Unthinkable," Sullivan's message suggested that the time had come for American officials to "examine some options which we have never before considered relevant." Sullivan noted that the shah had lost nearly all support among the Iranian people. He could probably hold on as long as the military continued to back him, but the military was becoming a question mark. The fundamentalist religious leaders had announced a campaign of passive resistance against the regime. The announcement created the potential for massive violence, if the generals ordered their men to shoot and the men obeyed, or the sudden collapse of the shah's regime, if the generals refused to give the order or the men refused to obey. After all that had happened at Jaleh Square and elsewhere, Sullivan found it hard to believe that the military would declare war on the Iranian people. The shah might soon be left with no support whatsoever. Sullivan's estimate of the situation caused him to assert that while the administration's current policy of backing the shah was "obviously the only safe course to pursue at this juncture," the policy ought to be carefully reviewed. "We need to think the unthinkable at this time in order to give our thoughts some precision should the unthinkable contingency arise."[20]

Sullivan's suggestion, tentative as it was, didn't produce much response in Washington. Carter was falling increasingly under the spell of Brzezinski and the hawks. Conservatives were battering him more mercilessly than ever, and Brzezinski had just about convinced him that to waver in support of the shah would be fatal to American credibility in much of the world—as well as to Carter's credibility in American politics. As a result, although some Middle East hands at the State Department pondered the possibility of cutting America loose from the shah, the pondering remained merely pondering, and it didn't materially alter the administration's policy.

Meanwhile the unrest in Iran intensified by the day. Strikes in protest of the shah's continued rule shut down whole sections of the economy, squeezing family budgets and causing shortages of all manner of consumer goods. Moderate, Western-oriented reformers

[20]Gary Sick, *All Fall Down* (New York, 1985), 81–83.

lost ground to the Islamic radicals as the influence of Ayatollah Khomeini increased. From exile in France, the elderly cleric demanded that the shah abdicate and that Iran be transformed into an Islamic republic. He sensed weakness in the shah, and he pressed his demands more uncompromisingly than ever. When one of his followers hinted that a gradual transition to Islamic rule might be better, Khomeini condemned the very idea. "No gradualism, no waiting," he thundered. "We must not lose a day, not a minute. The people demand an immediate revolution. Now or never."[21]

Yet even as Khomeini grew more confident of victory, Washington stuck by the shah. Part of the reason was that American intelligence regarding what was happening in Iran wasn't very good. Because American dealings with Iran had generally rated a low priority, few American foreign-service officers had devoted the time and energy required to master the Farsi language and to learn the nuances of Persian history and culture. As a result, although Americans like William Sullivan could see the turmoil at the surface of Iranian affairs, they had difficulty telling how deep the dissatisfaction with the shah went. Some unofficial American specialists in Iranian affairs warned of a possible cataclysm, but the people making the decisions didn't know whether the doomsayers were right or wrong. Nor did the shah help matters in this regard. He did his best to keep American officials from talking to members of the opposition. He also did his best to keep Americans from talking to his doctors; not until after his fall did Washington learn of his cancer.

A second reason for Washington's slowness to react was the Carter administration's preoccupation with other matters. Just as the crisis in Iran was coming to a head, the president and his top advisers were mounting their all-out push for a peace treaty between Israel and Egypt. With only one president and just twenty-four hours in a day, the United States government couldn't keep on top of everything happening in the world.

Besides, as Carter may have recognized, by this time there was little the United States could do to shape the outcome of events in Iran. The revolution there had gained too much momentum to be turned aside by Washington's wishes. Under such circumstances, Brzezinski's argument made fairly good sense: better to support the

[21]Rubin, *Paved with Good Intentions*, 222.

shah and gain a reputation for steadfastness than to abandon him and be known as irresolute.

Carter did continue to support the shah. At the end of October, the president told the shah's son, "Our friendship and our alliance with Iran is one of the important bases on which our entire foreign policy depends." In early December, the president asserted, "I fully expect the shah to maintain power in Iran." Carter added, "The shah has our support and he also has our confidence."[22]

But that support and confidence couldn't keep the shah on his throne. Increasingly debilitated by illness, and ever more uncertain of the loyalty of his army, the shah lost his nerve. In late December he appointed a new prime minister, the moderate Shahpour Bakhtiar, and in January he fled Iran for Egypt. Even at this late date, he may have entertained thoughts of returning. He recalled how he had left the country during the crisis of 1953 and returned following the (C.I.A.-assisted) outpouring of popular enthusiasm for his continued rule. Reportedly he now told Bakhtiar, just before getting on the plane, that the situation would deteriorate during the coming months and the people would call him back as they had before. For this reason, he refused to abdicate, as his opponents were demanding.

The shah's hope of returning proved to be the wishful thinking of a dying man. His departure only increased the momentum of the revolution, and within weeks Khomeini arrived triumphantly from exile aboard a specially chartered Air France 747. Amid the enthusiasm, Bakhtiar fell and power shifted toward the radicals.

The Carter administration made an eleventh-hour effort to limit the influence of Khomeini, whom it correctly perceived as bitterly anti-American. The president dispatched to Iran General Robert Huyser, the number-two man at America's European command headquarters and an individual with close personal connections to Iran's military. Huyser had orders from Carter to "urge military leaders to remain in Iran and to assure them that the United States would stick with them." American ambassador Sullivan had strong misgivings about Huyser's mission, fearing that it would only fan the flames of anti-Americanism that were rapidly consuming America's standing in Teheran. However, Sullivan hurt his case by com-

[22]Sick, *All Fall Down*, 62; *Public Papers*, Dec. 12, 1978.

ments and actions that sounded insubordinate to Washington, including a characterization of one presidential decision as "insane."[23]

Yet as matters turned out, Huyser would have been well advised to listen to Sullivan. The Iranian military leaders had no desire to put themselves any more in the way of the revolutionary juggernaut than they already were, and they kept their distance from Huyser and the Americans.

Indeed, as Sullivan had warned, the American efforts to stall the revolution reinforced Iranian suspicions. In Teheran and elsewhere there developed a widespread belief that the United States was plotting a restoration of the shah, on the pattern of the 1953 C.I.A. operation against Mussadiq. These suspicions caused many Iranians to view every American move as a possible precursor to an effort to return the shah to power.

Khomeini and the radicals manipulated these suspicions for their own benefit. Most revolutions need enemies. Until now, the shah had served quite well as the enemy of the Iranian revolution. After the shah departed, the United States, officially styled the "Great Satan," became the target of popular wrath. In such a situation, almost anything the Carter administration could have done would have exacerbated friction between Washington and the radicals in Teheran. For example, when American officials met with representatives of the Bakhtiar government and that of Bakhtiar's successor, Mehdi Bazargan, the mere fact of the meetings discredited those governments in the eyes of many Iranians. Nor did the American Senate improve the prospects of reconciliation when it passed a resolution denouncing the summary execution of certain persons associated with the shah's government. Regardless of the moral basis for such a resolution, most Iranians found it hard to interpret as other than hypocritical. The shah's secret police had tortured and murdered hundreds of innocent Iranians and the Senate had uttered nary a peep. Why now the great concern?

Khomeini and the Iranian radicals went out of their way to keep relations with the United States in an uproar. When one Khomeinist ventured the opinion that a particular proposed action might endanger the relationship with America, the ayatollah retorted, "May God cause it to be endangered. Our relations with the United States

[23]Sick, *All Fall Down*, 136–38.

are the relations of the oppressed with the oppressor. They are the relations of the plundered with the plunderer." Khomeini taunted, "What need have we of the United States?"[24]

Whether or not Khomeini *needed* the United States, he used it— to tar his rivals in Teheran. In February 1979, an armed crowd attacked the American embassy in Teheran. Ambassador Sullivan recognized that a vigorous defense of the embassy by the military guards would result in many casualties and additional Iranian hatred toward the United States. Consequently he ordered the surrender of the embassy to the attackers. They fatally shot one Iranian employed by the embassy and wounded an American marine. Then they took Sullivan and some one hundred other persons hostage.

Despite the two casualties, Sullivan's action soon appeared to have been prudent, for the hostages quickly regained their freedom. It turned out that the kidnappers were not Khomeinists but Marxists and others who wanted to pull the Iranian revolution in a leftward direction. Khomeini had as much disdain for the Marxists as for the shah and the Americans, although he had accepted the Marxists' cooperation in throwing out the shah. But now, with victory at hand, the ayatollah refused to let them in on the spoils. Shortly after the embassy takeover, Khomeini denounced the action. Before long the hostages were let loose and the Marxists went into eclipse.

In the autumn of 1979, a similar development yielded a decidedly different outcome. By then the Khomeinists were in a position to drive the last moderates from power. Searching for an incident to galvanize public opinion, the religious radicals found two—both incidents, not surprisingly, the result of actions by the Carter administration. One was a meeting in Algiers on November 1 between Brzezinski and Mehdi Bazargan. To the many Iranians predisposed to perceive diabolical manipulation in every American maneuver, the meeting appeared a precursor to an effort to reinstate the shah or otherwise frustrate the aspirations of the Iranian people.

The other incident was the admission of the shah to the United States for medical treatment. Numerous American officials warned against giving the shah a visa to enter America. Henry Precht of the State Department's Iran division had criticized the idea earlier. "Should the Shah come to the U.S., it would be a disaster for U.S.-Iranian relations, for the Western position in the region, and would

---

[24]Rubin, *Paved with Good Intentions*, 290.

create a severe security problem for our personnel in Tehran," Precht had written in March. In September, analysts at the embassy in Teheran prepared a report similarly forecasting trouble in case the shah entered the United States. "Any decision to allow him or his family to visit the U.S.," the embassy report asserted, "would almost certainly result in an immediate and violent reaction."[25]

Despite these misgivings, Carter went ahead and let the shah come to New York. To a certain extent, the president was merely offering assistance to a dying man in search of the best possible medical treatment. To a certain extent, Carter was responding to his conservative critics who insisted that the least the United States could do for a longtime ally was to let him come to America to gain a few more months of life. With the 1980 election only a year away, Carter didn't need any more criticism than he was already getting.

The news that the shah would be entering the United States sent shudders through the embassy in Teheran. One person there recalled the moment when the American chargé d'affaires relayed the report: "Total silence followed. In time it was broken by a faint groan. Faces literally went white. I put my hands over my own face and had a good think—not about policy or professional duties, but how much I wanted to go home."[26]

The desire to go home only increased during the next ten days. The Khomeinists derided the American statement that medical reasons accounted for the shah's visit, declaring that the Americans were plotting a counterrevolution. Khomeini demanded that the United States return the shah to Iran to face justice. Enormous crowds gathered outside the American embassy, shouting and waving their fists for the benefit of those inside the embassy and of the millions more watching on worldwide television. On November 4, a group of several hundred revolutionary enthusiasts scaled the walls of the embassy compound, overpowered the guards, and seized control of the place. More than seventy embassy personnel were taken hostage.

The Carter administration initially hoped for a swift solution to the crisis, on the order of the events of the previous February. This hope revealed Washington's misunderstanding of the change in Iranian politics during the interim. In the earlier case, Khomeini and

[25]James A. Bill, *The Eagle and the Lion* (New Haven, Conn., 1988), 323–24.
[26]Ibid., 326.

his followers had wanted to undermine the leftist hostage-takers and therefore had worked with the moderates in the government to secure the hostages' release. Now the Khomeinists wanted to undermine the government. Khomeini applauded the seizure of the embassy and elevated this batch of hostage-takers to the status of stalwarts of the Islamic revolution. When the kidnappers, with Khomeini's blessing, ignored the government's efforts to gain the release of the Americans, Bazargan's cabinet collapsed. The hardline Revolutionary Council took charge, and in a matter of weeks the Khomeinists succeeded in reconstitutionalizing Iran as an Islamic state.

At this point, his primary purpose accomplished, Khomeini might have ordered the American hostages freed. But by now he had discovered how potent the hostages were in guaranteeing bad feelings between Iran and the United States. Several days after the takeover of the embassy, Khomeini ordered the release of the African-Americans and women held, and later the captors let a sick hostage go. But the other fifty-two remained prisoners.

Carter inadvertently contributed to the hostages' value to Khomeini by making their release the central focus of his administration. He essentially imprisoned himself in the White House working on the Iranian problem. The American news media did their part by blaring headlines on the general theme of "America held hostage" and counting off the days since the beginning of the crisis. Carter's critics delighted in portraying him as helpless and ineffectual.

During the following weeks and then months, the administration employed various means to try to gain the hostages' freedom. Carter suspended deliveries of military spare parts to Iran and froze Iran's financial assets in the United States. The administration banned oil imports from Iran and deported Iranian students. It complained against Iran in the United Nations and sued Iran in the International Court of Justice. The president broke off diplomatic relations with Iran and declared an economic embargo. As soon as he could without appearing too ungracious or vacillating, Carter sent the shah away (to Panama, whence he traveled to Egypt to die in July 1980).

In April 1980, the president authorized a military rescue attempt. The plan was fraught with hazards, requiring the coordination of American ships, planes, and helicopters over long distances and in unfamiliar terrain. An American commando unit would fly to a site fifty miles from Teheran, then drive to the city under cover of darkness. The commandos would storm the embassy, grab the hostages, and take them to a stadium nearby, where they would be picked up by a squadron of helicopters.

Any number of things could go wrong; several did, even before the commandos got to Teheran. Mechanical malfunctions knocked out three helicopters, one of which collided with a transport plane, killing eight men. Carter had no choice but to abort the mission.

A political casualty of the rescue attempt was Cyrus Vance, who had opposed the effort as too risky. When Carter overruled his protests—and, in Vance's view, continued to fall under Brzezinski's spell—the secretary of state resigned in protest.

Another likely political casualty, as the 1980 election drew nearer and the hostages remained in Teheran, was the president himself.

5. A CRASH COURSE IN GEOPOLITICS

Cool-headed analysis of Carter's actions in the Iran hostage crisis suggested that the president was doing basically the right thing. With the one aberration of the rescue attempt, the president was patiently working for the hostages' release. To take strong military action against Iran, as numerous Carter critics were suggesting, might have been cathartically satisfying but would probably have resulted in the deaths of some or all of the hostages. With each day that they remained alive, the odds of their eventually coming home increased.

But cool heads can be scarce during a campaign season, and Carter's failure to resolve the hostage crisis weakened him politically. In doing so, it eroded his overall approach to foreign policy. By the beginning of 1980, Carter's approach couldn't stand much erosion. Denigrators of detente had been working Carter over for three years. The denigration wasn't strictly partisan: one of the most vocal critics of detente was Democratic senator Henry Jackson of Washington, who had reviled detente from the outset and called for a return to the militant anticommunist policies of the early Cold War. Like many opponents of detente, Jackson had mixed motives for his opposition. The presence of the Boeing aircraft company and other defense contractors in Jackson's home state contributed to his concern for strong defenses. In addition, Jackson had adopted Soviet Jews as his political wards; the 1975 Jackson-Vanik amendment—sponsored in the House of Representatives by Charles Vanik—conditioned most-favored-nation trade status for the Soviet Union on increased opportunities for emigration by Soviet Jews. When Moscow refused to accept what it considered American dictation on internal Soviet matters, Jackson did his best to worsen relations between the two countries. (A joke that made the rounds in Moscow at this time captured both the Soviets' feelings about American meddling and the bleak conditions of life in the U.S.S.R. The top Soviet leaders Brezhnev and Alexei Kosygin are talking about the American demands. "If we let as many people go as the Americans want," Brezhnev says to Kosygin, "there won't be anyone left here but you and me." "Speak for yourself, Leonid," Kosygin replies.)

The intellectual attack on detente was even more significant than the narrowly political attack. During the mid-1970s, a group of former leftists, including some refugees from the American Communist party, banded together under the label of "neoconservatism." The neoconservatives exhibited diverse views on American domestic affairs, but regarding international relations they concurred that communism was the overriding threat to American interests and world peace. Detente was a snare and a delusion—for the United States, not for the Soviet Union, which continued to promote its totalitarian agenda under the cloak of peaceful coexistence.

The neoconservatives despised Jimmy Carter. They judged him fuzzy-minded in the philosophy of foreign affairs and ineffectual in its implementation. They interpreted his warning against an inordinate fear of communism as revealing a stunning naiveté about the world, and they lampooned his interest in human rights as school-marmishly unrealistic.

Carter had silenced his critics briefly during 1978 with his successful mediation between Israel and Egypt, but the developments of 1979 and 1980 set the critics screaming once again. The triumph of radical revolutionaries in Iran and Nicaragua seemed to the neoconservatives to prove what the muddleheaded policies of the Carter administration inevitably led to.

In November 1979, a withering and widely noticed assault on Carter by political scientist Jeane Kirkpatrick appeared in *Commentary* magazine, the chief organ of neoconservatism, summarizing the neoconservative case against the president. Entitled "Dictators and

Double Standards," the article accused Carter of treating America's allies worse than he treated America's enemies. Kirkpatrick asserted that Carter's policies toward the shah and Somoza, two rulers who though imperfect were far better than those certain to follow, could hardly have been more misguided. "In each country," Kirkpatrick declared, "the Carter administration not only failed to prevent the undesired outcome, it actively collaborated in the replacement of moderate autocrats friendly to American interests with less friendly autocrats of extremist persuasion."

Kirkpatrick distinguished between authoritarians of the right, like the shah and Somoza, and totalitarians of the left, such as the rulers of most communist states. Right-wing authoritarians, she said, contented themselves with monopolizing political power, leaving individuals' lives more or less alone, while left-wing totalitarians insinuated themselves into all aspects of individual existence. More crucially, right-wing authoritarianism was susceptible to reformist influences, while left-wing totalitarianism was essentially irredeemable. "Although there is no instance of a revolutionary 'socialist' or Communist society being democratized," Kirkpatrick wrote, "right-wing autocracies do sometimes evolve into democracies—given time, propitious economic, social and political circumstances, talented leaders, and a strong indigenous demand for representative government." The Carter administration's chief crime in Iran and Nicaragua was to destabilize right-wing authoritarians who also happened to be friendly to the United States, and assist in their replacement by regimes of decidedly totalitarian tendencies.[27]

Only a month after Kirkpatrick's article appeared, an event occurred in Central Asia that seemed to clinch the neoconservative case against Carter. Since the nineteenth century, Afghanistan had served as center court in the "great game" between Britain and Russia. The Russians tried to push southward toward the Persian Gulf and India, while the British tried to hold the Russians back. Because the Afghans were such ferocious fighters, neither the Russians nor the British ever controlled much of Afghanistan for long.

After World War II, the game changed. Britain pulled out of India (including what became Pakistan), and the Russians concentrated on consolidating their grip in other areas, particularly Eastern

---

[27]Jeane Kirkpatrick, "Dictatorships and Double Standards," *Commentary*, November 1979.

Europe. Afghanistan joined the ranks of the nonaligned states, tied to neither Moscow nor Washington in the Cold War. Gradually, though, closer relations developed between the Soviet Union and Afghanistan. The Kremlin began shipping weapons to the Afghan government, then advisers and technicians. By the late 1970s, Moscow and Kabul were on comparatively cozy terms. Afghanistan remained nominally nonaligned, but the government of Mohammad Daoud Khan tilted noticeably toward the Kremlin.

Unfortunately for the Kremlin and Daoud, the Afghan leader had many enemies, some of whom combined forces to topple him in April 1978. To emphasize their dissatisfaction with Daoud's style of governing, the coup makers massacred Daoud's whole family and the families of his chief assistants. Yet this chapter of the story had a reasonably happy ending from Moscow's perspective, in that the new rulers in Kabul, Nur Mohammad Taraki and Hafizullah Amin, indicated interest in keeping up the friendly ties to the Soviet Union.

Taraki and Amin, however, soon ran afoul of Islamic radicals, theological kin to the Islamists who were busy overthrowing the shah in next-door Iran. The Islamic radicals launched a holy war against the Taraki regime. Amid the fighting and confusion, terrorists kidnapped and killed the American ambassador in Kabul. In September 1979, Taraki went down, although not at the hands of the rebels. He was done in by his partner Amin, who preferred to rule by himself.

The Soviets were as worried about the situation in Afghanistan as the Americans were about events in Iran—more so, in fact, to judge by subsequent events. The Kremlin allowed Amin a few months to stifle the revolt, but he succeeded no better than Taraki had. Soviet leaders grew increasingly nervous that the religious radicalism that was gaining ascendancy in Iran would sweep over Afghanistan and into the Soviet Union's largely Muslim Central Asian republics. Moscow viewed the seizure of the American embassy in Teheran with ambivalence: with pleasure in that it discomfited Washington, but with distress for what it portended for the stability of the Central Asian region.

In the last week of December 1979, the Kremlin decided that Amin needed help in strangling the revolt in Afghanistan. Moscow ordered a massive airlift of troops over the mountains into Afghanistan, and tanks and other support quickly followed by land. Though the Russians claimed that Amin had invited them in, he became one of the first casualties of the intervention. His replacement, Babrak Karmal, announced that Amin had not been what he claimed to be. Rather, he was a "charlatan of history" and a "bloodthirsty agent of American imperialism." The Soviet newspaper *Pravda* reported the verdict at the beginning of 1980: "Overthrown by a wave of popular indignation, the treacherous scoundrel was tried and shot."[28]

To the Carter administration, the Soviet invasion of Afghanistan came as an eye-opener. The effect was especially marked on the doves in the administration. Vance commented later that the invasion was "unquestionably a severe setback to the policy I advocated." Carter told an interviewer, "My opinion of the Russians has changed more drastically in the last week than in the two and one-half years before that." Brzezinski, who had expected such things from the Kremlin all along, afterward recalled his feeling that the affair represented a "major watershed" in Soviet-American relations.[29]

The potential repercussions of the Soviet invasion were daunting. At a minimum, the invasion would further damage Carter's credibility in foreign affairs. For three years the president had been telling the American people not to worry so much about the Soviets, while his critics had been saying that the president had better worry more. By sending tens of thousands of troops (eventually some one hundred thousand) into Afghanistan, Moscow appeared to be proving the critics right and the president wrong.

Adding to the domestic political impact of the Soviet invasion of Afghanistan was another big jump in oil prices. This second "oil shock" had started rocking the industrial world during the shah's last months in Iran, when oil workers walked off their jobs in Iran's oil fields and refineries. Within weeks, the strikers paralyzed the country's oil industry almost completely. Iran recently had been the world's second-largest oil exporter, and the shutdown caused a panic in world markets. Purchasing agents bid prices up from thirteen dollars per barrel to thirty-four. Gas lines reappeared on the streets of America, triggering violence in a few neighborhoods and bad tempers in all. Although prices eased somewhat during the first half of 1979, as the oil strikers celebrated the shah's ouster by re-

[28]Adam B. Ulam, *Dangerous Relations* (New York, 1983), 256–57.
[29]Vance, *Hard Choices*, 394; *American Foreign Policy*, 811–12; Zbigniew Brzezinski, *Power and Principle* (New York, 1983), 429.

turning to work, the November seizure of the American embassy and the December Soviet invasion of Afghanistan sent another series of shock waves through the international markets. Spot cargoes commanded as much as forty-five dollars per barrel. Inflation leaped again, and what Carter's critics had lately labeled the "misery index"—the combination of inflation and unemployment—topped previous highs.

The possible geopolitical implications of the Soviet invasion of Afghanistan were even more alarming than the political and economic ones. If the move into Afghanistan portended a Soviet thrust toward the Persian Gulf, the United States might soon find the principal source of oil for the American alliance system at severe risk. Every U.S. president since 1945 had taken as a primary task preventing such a scenario. Carter could do no less.

As a first response to the invasion, Carter called Brezhnev on the direct White House–Kremlin line and proclaimed the Soviet move "a clear threat to the peace" and potentially "a fundamental and long-lasting turning point in our relations." The president went on to say, "Unless you draw back from your present course of action, this will inevitably jeopardize the course of United States–Soviet relations throughout the world. I urge you to take prompt constructive action to withdraw your forces and cease interference in Afghanistan's internal affairs."[30]

When the Kremlin ignored this demand, Carter went public with a major policy declaration. He commandeered national television time to label the Soviet invasion of Afghanistan "the greatest threat to peace since the Second World War." Defining what quickly came to be called the Carter Doctrine, the president asserted that the United States would vigorously oppose additional advances by the Soviets. "An attempt by any outside force to gain control of the Persian Gulf region," he said, "will be regarded as an assault on the vital interests of the United States of America, and such an assault will be repelled by any means necessary, including military force."

To put muscle into his statement, Carter ordered the establishment of a special military unit, the Rapid Deployment Force, which would be specifically designed to respond on short notice to dangers to the safety of the Persian Gulf. In addition, he withdrew the as yet unratified SALT II treaty from consideration by the Senate, reinsti-

[30]Carter, *Keeping Faith*, 472.

tuted registration for the military draft, barred sales of grain and high-technology products to the Soviet Union, ordered an American boycott of the 1980 Moscow summer Olympics, and requested the first big increase in American defense spending since the Vietnam War.[31]

Carter's reversal of course after the Soviet invasion of Afghanistan indicated the evanescence of idealism in American foreign policy. Americans initially had followed the Democratic president in embracing the notion that the United States could aspire to higher standards than it had practiced during much of the Cold War. Most were pleased at his emphasis on human rights, which if not enormously successful in changing the ways of repressive regimes at least distanced the United States from the worst of the repression. And nearly all applauded his accomplishments regarding Israel and Egypt. Though not strictly a triumph for idealism, the Camp David accords and the subsequent Egypt-Israel peace treaty demonstrated what could be done to defuse regional disputes by an administration not obsessed with the superpower struggle.

But the trouble with idealism, as practiced in American politics, is that it asks too much of the world too fast. American politics is the art of the here and now. Voters have short memories; policies that can't deliver their objectives within months get shoved aside by those that promise faster results.

Carter's idealistic approach might have succeeded if given time. It probably wouldn't have made the Soviet leaders nicer people; it doubtless wouldn't have disposed Ayatollah Khomeini more favorably toward the United States. But if pursued consistently for several years it might have established a credible American reputation for integrity and fair-mindedness in international relations. Those foreign governments that expected Washington to lose interest in their abuse of their citizens would have had to adapt to new circumstances. Contestants in regional quarrels might have come to look on the United States as an honest—not to mention powerful—broker. Revolutionaries in foreign countries would have had to find other Satans to rally the faithful against. To change the world is not impossible; to do so overnight is.

Carter's idealism didn't get the time it needed. Ridiculed from

[31]*Weekly Compilation of Presidential Documents*, Jan. 14 and 28, 1980.

the start by those who longed for the old verities of the Cold War, it gained additional opponents with each jolt to the global status quo. To the extent that the revolutions in Nicaragua and Iran were anti-American, they were so in reaction to previous American policies, not those of the Carter administration. Yet with the Sandinistas spitting revilement of Yankee imperialism and the Khomeinists holding American hostages, that was a finer distinction than most Americans were able to make. In the clamor that accompanied the approaching American elections, distinctions grew still more difficult.

Detente likely would have died even had the Soviets not invaded Afghanistan. Indeed, to the extent it considered possible American reactions to its move, the Kremlin may well have decided that detente would be unmentionable in America by November 1980 and therefore not worth trying to preserve. Long study had clued Soviet Americanologists in to the short-term bias in American electoral politics.

Carter didn't help matters by his eleventh-hour apostasy from idealism and his conversion to Cold War realpolitik. But as the president himself understood—and if he hadn't understood, the news broadcasts tallying up the number of days the hostages had been locked away in Iran would have forced understanding upon him—events were moving beyond his control.

CHAPTER 3

The New Cold War: 1980–1984

Another trouble with idealism is that it is hard to explain. Any father knows that when Johnny comes home with a black eye, the easy thing to do is to give him a couple of boxing lessons and tell him to punch the jerk's lights out the next time he comes looking for a fight. More difficult is to preach forbearance in the broader interest of schoolyard order. (The dynamics are different when Sally comes home with a black eye. But then, to date, few foreign policy decisions have been made by the Sallys and their mothers of the world. Which may explain why they've been made the way they have. Or it may not.)

A concomitant of the short-term bias in American politics is the repeatedly demonstrated fact that simplicity sells. Most Americans don't care deeply about foreign affairs; the more pressing matters of their daily lives consume the great majority of their energy and interest. Wars and smaller crises intrude now and then, and in such cases the masses can't help responding. But the patient attention required for dealing with international affairs between crises is usually lacking. And the more patience that is required of a given policy, the more likely it is to be lacking. Complicated, slow-acting policies usually require the most patience; therefore they are the least likely to succeed for long.

The policies Americans had supported during most of the Cold War were based on an exceedingly simple idea: that the Soviet Union and communism were the wellsprings of evil in the world and must be opposed at nearly any cost. Detente complicated matters by treating the Soviet Union as something less than an implacable foe and by contending that communists could be worthwhile partners for Americans. Carter's concern for human rights and poverty amelioration complicated things further by extending the definition of American interests to include the liberty and happiness of people in potentially every country on earth.

In the early 1980s Americans rejected the complications of Nixonian detente and Carterist idealism in favor of a simple reformulation of the original Cold War ideology. Many observers perceived in Ronald Reagan's enormous popularity a nostalgia for times when heroes wore white, villains wore black, and women and children stayed home and off the streets. It wasn't accidental that Reagan's emergence coincided with a vogue for the 1950s—or rather for the 1950s as they were fondly remembered: an unambiguous golden age of unquestioned American virtue and unchallenged American power.

Reagan indulged Americans in their nostalgia. He called for America to "stand tall" once again, and he directed a large military buildup to help the country do so. He branded the Soviet Union an "evil empire" and blamed the communists for nearly all the bad things happening in the world. The Soviet occupation of Afghanistan, to the Reaganite way of thinking, was merely the most visible manifestation of Moscow's malevolent designs. Unrest in Central America was the work of Moscow's agents and stooges. Likewise trouble in central Africa. In Southeast Asia, Soviet ally Vietnam was creating a communist Indochinese empire. In each of these areas, the Reagan administration endeavored to reverse the radicals' gains by supporting rightist guerrilla groups. As for the Middle East, if the Kremlin hadn't created the trouble between the Arabs and Israel, and among the Arabs themselves, Soviet policies certainly exacerbated the turbulence in that chronically restless region. The United States needed to step in to restore such calm as was possible.

Reagan's approach to the world was at once unnerving and comforting. It was unnerving in that it portrayed the communists as incredibly energetic and clever. They were active the world over, and where they themselves weren't spearheading activities inimical to liberty and world peace, they had duped others into doing their work for them. Reagan's approach was comforting in that it greatly simplified what had seemed so complex for most of the 1970s. Since Vietnam, Americans had been trying to adjust to the idea that the straightforward bipolar world order of the first quarter century of the Cold War had been replaced by a more complicated and less manageable structure. Reagan asserted that the bipolar order was alive and well—or rather, alive and under as serious threat from communist machinations as ever.

1. THE REAGAN REVIVAL

Like Jimmy Carter (and nearly all other U.S. presidents), Ronald Reagan was elected for primarily domestic reasons. As in most presidential elections, the condition of the American economy counted far more heavily in voters' thinking than the state of the world abroad. Yet again as with the election of 1976, foreign affairs slipped in the back door of the White House with the new tenant. The economic woes Carter got blamed for in the campaign were magnified, if not entirely created, by confusion overseas. The oil shocks of 1973 and 1979 were still working their way through the U.S. economy, pushing prices up and employment down. Though Carter, by his mediation between Israel and Egypt, had done more than any other American president to calm the turmoil in the Middle East, the domestic economic costs of the trouble there got charged against his account. More dramatically, the continued captivity of the American hostages in Iran made Carter appear weak. Many Americans looked for strong leadership from the White House to remedy their country's ills; with the Iranian hostage-holders making rude gestures at America nightly on the news, Carter didn't seem quite the person to provide it.

Reagan won in November 1980 primarily because he wasn't the incumbent; but he also won because he promised a return to the certainties that had undergirded American thinking about the world during the glory days of the first twenty-five years after 1945. With Reagan, it was impossible to know just how much he really believed of the simplicity he preached, and how much was an act—the crowning role of his career. At times he obviously knew more than he let on. In his first inaugural address he told a tale about Martin Treptow, an American soldier from World War I who had been killed in action but left behind a diary containing what he called "My Pledge": "America must win this war. Therefore I will work, I will save, I will sacrifice, I will endure, I will fight cheerfully and do my utmost, as if the issue of the whole struggle depended on me alone." When Reagan had first heard the story, it moved him to tears, and he couldn't resist including it in his inaugural. As a dramatic flourish, he motioned from the west steps of the Capitol across the mall and across the Potomac to Arlington National Cemetery—"with its row upon row of simple white markers bearing crosses or Stars of David." Reagan concluded the story: "Under one such marker lies a young man, Martin Treptow." Actually, Reagan knew full well that Martin Treptow wasn't buried at Arlington but in Wisconsin; his fact checkers had told him so. But he also knew that it made a better punch line to inter the hero of his story across the river from the inauguration proceedings.[1]

In other areas Reagan's ignorance was clearly unfeigned. Only after two years in office did he learn that the principal element of the Soviet nuclear arsenal consisted of land-based intercontinental missiles. In response to a reporter's question as to how such a basic piece of information—which was known to any lay person who read newspapers even occasionally, and which certainly ought to have been known by someone who had been warning against Soviet nuclear capabilities for years—had escaped him, he replied, "I never heard anyone of our negotiators or any of our military people or anyone else bring up that particular point." No less an authority than Richard Nixon found Reagan's ignorance downright scary. Following a 1987 briefing with Reagan on upcoming arms control talks with Soviet head Mikhail Gorbachev, the former president confided to a private memo: "There is no way he can ever be allowed to participate in a private meeting with Gorbachev."[2]

But well-informed or not, Reagan insisted on a return to traditional American policies. He called for a revival of the containment policy of the early Cold War. The communists had never stopped trying to subvert the Free World, he contended, and the Free World should never have stopped combatting the subversion. Reagan accepted the neoconservative criticism of detente: that it amounted to a unilateral cease-fire which the communists constantly exploited. He pledged to reverse detente and resume the fight against Soviet subversion. The fact that Carter had abandoned detente almost a year before the election only improved Reagan's chances of defeating him. Having embraced detente for three years, Carter was poorly placed to attack it. Reagan could do so far more convincingly.

[1]*Public Papers of the Presidents: Reagan,* Jan. 20, 1981; Lou Cannon, *President Reagan* (New York, 1991), 99–100.
[2]Cannon, *President Reagan,* 291; Jonathan Aitken, *Nixon* (Washington, 1993), 562.

The policy Reagan proposed to replace detente with was containment—but containment with a difference. Reagan's version entailed large military expenditures, as the containment of the early 1950s had done. Picking up from Carter's last-year conversion to a big military, Reagan requested and Congress approved record budgets for the Pentagon. Between fiscal 1981 and 1985, American defense spending leaped 34 percent in real (inflation-adjusted) terms. The Pentagon found itself awash in funds. The admirals laid plans and keels for a six-hundred-ship navy, recently nothing more than a dream. The generals of the air force ordered long-range bombers, radar-invisible fighters, and laser-guided bombs, by the dozens and hundreds. The army generals bought trainloads of tanks that were faster and more powerful than anyone else's, arsenals of ordnance that was unprecedently destructive, and assorted state-of-the-art gadgetry that would make American combat soldiers veritable bionic men.

The big military buildup had two objectives, one openly stated and the other sometimes not. The less acknowledged objective was the recovery of the American economy. The recovery didn't begin at once, and in fact the first two years of Reagan's first term witnessed a wrenching recession. But the wrenching squeezed most of the inflation out of the system, and beginning in late 1982 the American economy entered a protracted period of steady growth. The country's gross domestic product (the sum of the goods produced and services rendered throughout the country) climbed every year through the end of the Reagan administration. Unemployment correspondingly declined. The administration's defense buildup wasn't entirely responsible for the economic recovery, but the huge injection of government spending into an important sector of the economy played a substantial role. (That the increased spending was uncompensated for by a comparable increase in taxes gave the shot in the arm much of its potency. In this respect the early 1980s reflected the early 1960s, when at the urging of the Kennedy administration Congress expanded defense spending while trimming taxes.) Profits and employment in the defense industry jumped sharply during Reagan's first term, and those profits and the wages generated by that employment spilled over into other parts of the economy.

The second, openly avowed objective of the Reagan military buildup was the awing of America's international rivals. Foremost among these rivals was the Soviet Union, but other potential troublemakers were supposed to get the message as well. The message was that the post-Vietnam era of American self-doubt was over. The United States was once again willing and able to defend its interests around the globe.

Or at least able. As events soon proved, the Reagan buildup was essentially for show. This didn't by itself make the buildup unimportant as a deterrent to bad behavior: the gun that never leaves the holster serves a purpose if it frightens the outlaws into leaving town. But frightening, rather than compelling, was the heart of the Reagan strategy. Despite some loose talk among Reaganite armchair strategists about the possibility of meaningful victory in a nuclear war, the Republican president steered well clear of anything that might actually have required the serious use of all the new planes, ships, and guns.

On the two occasions when Soviet actions provided a plausible pretext for bold reactions, Reagan moved cautiously. The first occasion was the suppression of the opposition Solidarity movement in Poland in December 1981. Though the suppression was directly the work of the Polish military, no one had any doubt that General Wojciech Jaruzelski and his colleagues had the blessing of Moscow. After years of excoriating the Kremlin for just such crimes against freedom, and of rebuking Democrats and detente-minded Republicans for condoning such behavior, Reagan confined himself to comparatively gentle gestures of American displeasure. And even these were targeted chiefly against hapless Poland rather than the Soviet Union. Sanctions against the Soviets were confined to a denial of landing privileges to the Soviet airline Aeroflot, restrictions on certain purchasing practices by Soviet industry, delay of some grain sales, curbs on shipments of high-tech equipment, and the nonrenewal of a scientific exchange agreement.

The administration did not suspend arms control negotiations, walk out of human rights talks then under way, or cancel a scheduled meeting between Secretary of State Alexander Haig and Soviet foreign minister Andrei Gromyko. And within months, it was stroking the wrist it had so softly slapped. By the following summer, American grain was again being loaded for Soviet destinations and new contracts were being written for advanced industrial machinery.

The second opportunity for an energetic American response to a Soviet sin occurred in September 1983, when a Soviet fighter plane shot down a Korean airliner that had strayed into Russian airspace, killing all aboard. Reagan denounced the downing as an act of cold-blooded barbarism. The president claimed that the Soviets had known the airliner was a civilian plane but had blasted it anyway, and thereby committed mass murder. Yet despite the name-calling, the administration again confined itself primarily to another suspension of Aeroflot flights to the United States.

For the first few years of the Reagan presidency, the administration's striking combination of affinity for strong gestures and aversion to strong action seemed mostly an ad hoc affair. But in 1984 Reagan's defense secretary, Caspar Weinberger, outlined a general philosophy regarding the circumstances under which the United States might resort to a particular form of strong action—the use of military force. Weinberger's statement was the first comprehensive attempt by a top American official in the post-Vietnam era to define the conditions under which American military force would be appropriate. Predictably, the conditions Weinberger described reflected the Vietnam experience.

The defense secretary listed six criteria. First, troops should be committed to combat only in situations "vital to our national interest or that of our allies." Second, the government must be so sure of the interests at stake that it would allow the troops to fight "wholeheartedly and with the clear intention of winning." If the troops weren't supposed to win, they shouldn't be committed. Third, the objectives of the deployment must be "clearly defined" and American leaders must see "precisely how our forces can accomplish those clearly defined objectives." Fourth, Washington must constantly be alert to changing circumstances. "Conditions and objectives invariably change during the course of a conflict. When they do change, then so must our combat requirements. We must continuously keep as a beacon light before us the basic questions: 'Is this conflict in our national interest? Does our national interest require us to fight, to use force of arms?'" Fifth, the president must have "some reasonable assurance" of the support of the American public and Congress. "We cannot fight a battle with the Congress at home while asking our troops to win a war oversees, or, as in the case of Vietnam, in effect asking our troops not to win, but just to be there." Sixth, military action should be a "last resort." All other avenues must be exhausted before the troops were dispatched.[3]

Weinberger's wasn't the only opinion on the subject of when military force was appropriate. Somewhat ironically—although not surprisingly, considering the American military's searing experience in Vietnam—the defense secretary was far less forward about the use of American troops than were the Reagan administration's top diplomats. Perhaps Weinberger's philosophy would have been better received in the State Department had former general Alexander Haig remained secretary of state for long. But Haig was a hard man to deal with, and certain parties in the White House doubted his judgment, even rationality. On one memorable occasion, after an aspiring assassin shot Reagan, Haig rushed to the White House briefing room to announce before the television cameras: "I am in control here." Haig's explanation—that with the president on the operating table and the vice president out of town, he was next in the line of authority—was lost in the frenzy of the moment and the distraught appearance of Haig himself. Besides, his explanation was wrong: the speaker of the House of Representatives and the president pro tem of the Senate precede the secretary of state in constitutional order of succession. Treasury secretary Donald Regan couldn't believe his eyes and ears. "What's this all about?" he demanded. "Is he mad?" Defense secretary Weinberger wondered the same thing. "I can't believe this," Weinberger said. "He's wrong; he doesn't have any such authority." C.I.A. director William Casey declared, "This is unbelievable."[4]

Haig survived this fiasco but not many more, and in June 1982 he was replaced by George Shultz. Almost from the start the new secretary of state disputed Weinberger's philosophy of the use of military force. Shultz thought the Pentagon was altogether too cautious with its hardware. He conceded that diplomatic solutions to problems of American foreign relations were usually preferable to miliary solutions, but he contended that the credible threat of military force made diplomatic solutions easier to find. "Americans have sometimes tended to think that power and diplomacy are two distinct alternatives," Shultz said. "This reflects a fundamental misunderstanding. The truth is: power and diplomacy must always go together, or we

[3] *American Foreign Policy: Current Documents 1984*, 65–70.
[4] Donald T. Regan, *For the Record* (New York, 1988), 186.

will accomplish very little in this world. Power must always be guided by purpose. At the same time, the hard reality is that diplomacy not backed by strength will always be ineffectual at best, dangerous at worst." Against Weinberger's six points, Shultz opposed three. American military force was legitimate when, first, "it can help liberate a people or support the yearning for freedom"; second, "its aim is to bring peace or to support peaceful processes"; and third, "it is applied with the greatest efforts to avoid unnecessary casualties and with a conscience troubled by the pain unavoidably inflicted."[5]

Reagan usually sided with Weinberger in this debate, but not always. Only once during his eight years in office did the Republican president send American troops deliberately into battle. In October 1983, Reagan ordered the invasion of the tiny Caribbean island-nation of Grenada. The invasion followed a long series of administration warnings of trouble brewing in Grenada. The left-leaning prime minister, Maurice Bishop, had been actively pursuing closer ties to Cuba and the Soviet Union. Reagan described Bishop's actions as evidence of "the tightening grip of the totalitarian left in Grenada." When Moscow and Havana assisted Bishop's government to expand the island's airport and in particular to build a new long runway, Reagan asked, "Who is it for?" The president thought he knew the answer: for the Soviets, who would use the airport as an air base. Reagan dismissed Bishop's rejoinder that the airport expansion was to accommodate long-range airliners bringing tourists who would bolster Grenada's sagging economy. Reagan publicly deplored what he called the "rapid buildup of Grenada's military potential," which he declared to be "unrelated to any conceivable threat." He summarized, "The Soviet-Cuban militarization of Grenada, in short, can only be seen as power projection into the region."[6]

As much as Reagan worried about Bishop, he took genuine alarm when Bishop was overthrown by individuals evidently more radical still. The new regime was dominated by what Reagan labeled "a brutal gang of leftist thugs." In order to consolidate its position, the regime did indeed impose a variety of harsh measures. Among these was what the president branded, with comparatively minor editorializing, as a "barbaric shoot-to-kill curfew."[7]

[5]Department of State *Bulletin*, February 1984.
[6]*Public Papers*, Feb. 24, 1982, and Mar. 23, 1983.
[7]*New York Times*, Oct. 26, 1983; *Public Papers*, Oct. 25, 1983.

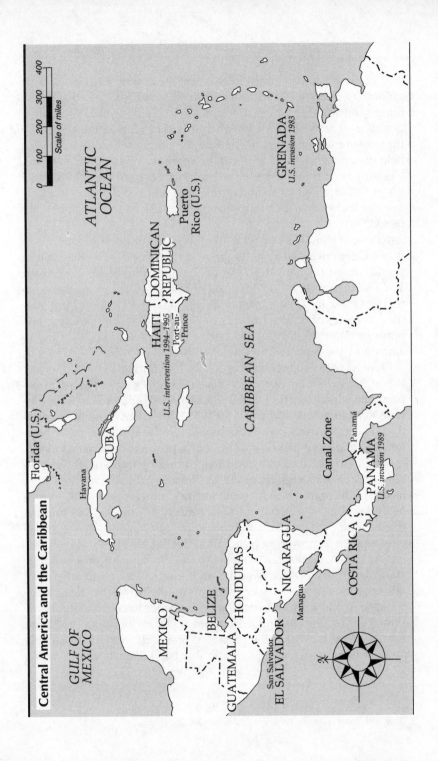

Central America and the Caribbean

GULF OF MEXICO

Florida (U.S.)

Havana

CUBA

MEXICO

BELIZE

GUATEMALA

San Salvador
EL SALVADOR

HONDURAS

NICARAGUA

Managua

COSTA RICA

PANAMA
U.S. invasion 1989

Panamá

Canal Zone

CARIBBEAN SEA

HAITI
U.S. intervention 1994–1995

Port-au-Prince

DOMINICAN REPUBLIC

Puerto Rico (U.S.)

ATLANTIC OCEAN

GRENADA
U.S. invasion 1983

Scale of miles

0 100 200 300 400

The threat of widespread violence provided Reagan the justification he desired for turning the situation in Grenada around. Several hundred American medical students were studying in St. George's, the capital, and the administration quickly made a case that the unrest on the island threatened these American kids and therefore required a strong response. An airlift evacuation might have sufficed, but the president chose an invasion instead. Before most Americans had time to locate Grenada in their atlases, Reagan ordered six thousand marines ashore.

The operation succeeded swiftly, although not as swiftly as many military analysts thought it should have. The administration declared a great victory for the legions of freedom and handed out ribbons by the armload to the officers and troops. Persons inside and outside the administration who hoped to rehabilitate military power as an instrument of American foreign policy declared—quite prematurely, as it turned out—that the shadow of Vietnam had been lifted from the American psyche.

The Grenada operation was an exception that proved the rule of the Reagan's administration's reluctance to use military force. In general, the president preferred to let other people do the Free World's fighting for it. This policy of proxy warfare eventually was dignified with the sobriquet "Reagan Doctrine," but it amounted to little more than an assertion that where left-wing governments mistreated their people, right-wing insurgents might act as agents of U.S. interests. American conservatives had long complained that the communists had cornered the market on subversion. Radical insurgents undermined conservative governments around the world, but radical governments weren't confronted with conservative insurgencies. This complaint was overstated, as anyone familiar with American covert operations in Iran, Guatemala, Cuba, Chile, and various other countries from the 1950s to the 1970s knew. Yet it wasn't entirely wrong, and Reagan set out to rectify the imbalance.

The most successful, if slow, application of the Reagan Doctrine was to Afghanistan. As the Soviet army settled in for what looked likely to be a protracted war against the Afghans, the Reagan administration provided the Afghan resistance, the mujahideen, with covert military aid. Initially the aid consisted chiefly of small arms and ammunition, which did little to deter the Soviets and their Afghan allies from wrecking the country and massacring many civilians. But gradually Washington stepped up the caliber of its assistance, and when it started sending the mujahideen Stinger missiles (shoulder-launched ground-to-air rockets), which soon began blasting Soviet aircraft out of the sky, the odds in the fight for Afghanistan drew more even. After almost as long as the United States required to recognize that it wasn't going to win in Vietnam, the Kremlin (under new leadership) in 1988 decided to cut its losses and leave Afghanistan for the Afghans to fight over (which they proceeded to do through the mid-1990s).

The Afghanistan theater in the new Cold War provided a good illustration of the difference in recent American foreign policy between "covert" actions and "secret" actions. No one who cared could miss the fact that the United States was providing arms and money to the mujahideen; yet, for the international record, the Reagan administration refused to acknowledge the supply operation. The major reason for this diplomatic charade was that an open admission of the program would have embarrassed Pakistan, through which most of the aid was flowing. The Pakistanis didn't want to provoke the Kremlin into attacking them, but neither did they want the American aid to stop, since Pakistani middlemen and the Pakistan government were raking off a sizable cut. The Kremlin knew what was going on but didn't desire to add to its problems by widening the war into Pakistan. Besides, the Soviets would have felt their credibility was more squarely on the line if the United States had publicly acknowledged its role in the supply program. The easiest way out for everyone was for Washington to maintain the fiction that it wasn't involved.

The Reagan Doctrine policy of arming right-wing guerrillas ("freedom fighters," in the lexicon of the administration and its friends) against left-wing governments gave rise to similar supply operations in Angola, Cambodia, and Nicaragua. In Angola, the Reagan administration achieved what Congress had denied to the Ford administration in terms of covert aid. In doing so, the Reaganites widened the civil war that had been under way since the mid-1970s. The Reagan administration's hero in Angola was Jonas Savimbi, the leader of the opposition UNITA and the sworn foe of the leftist government of Eduardo dos Santos. Savimbi wasn't quite such a hero to critics of the Reagan administration, many of whom faulted the UNITA leader for his alliance with the apartheid government of South Africa and for various atrocities related to UNITA's prosecution of the war. Yet during the early years of the

Reagan ascendancy, the critics had little effect on American foreign policy, and the aid flowed. It proved insufficient to allow UNITA to drive dos Santos from power, but it did keep the civil war going and dos Santos somewhat off balance. (The war was still going on in the mid-1990s.)

If Savimbi's actions made some Americans queasy, the activities of other beneficiaries of the Reagan Doctrine made them downright ill. In 1978, Vietnam had invaded Cambodia (also called Kampuchea) to overthrow the insanely homicidal Khmer Rouge regime, which had presided over the murder of perhaps a million Cambodians, and to establish Hanoi's primacy in Indochina. Although the overthrow of the Khmer Rouge almost certainly improved the prospects (most basically, the average life expectancy) of the Cambodian people, the United States government protested the invasion. Washington's protests were partly an effort to uphold the inviolability of international borders, partly a way of opposing the extension of communist rule, and partly sour grapes by the losing side in the Vietnam War. Under the Reagan administration, the United States sent covert aid to a Cambodian coalition dedicated to driving the Vietnamese out. The best-organized group within the coalition was none other than the Khmer Rouge. The administration conceded the risks involved in this application of the Reagan Doctrine, but it hoped that if and when the Vietnamese were forced out of Cambodia, other elements of the coalition would prevent the Khmer Rouge from resuming their murderous ways. (By the mid-1990s the Vietnamese had left, as much for their own reasons as from American pressure; the future of the Khmer Rouge remained up in the air.)

2. THE WAR FOR CENTRAL AMERICA

Even more controversial than Cambodia as a theater of the new Cold War was Nicaragua. Although Congress had followed the Carter administration's lead in approving the $75 million aid package during the spring of 1980, relations between Washington and Managua soon resumed their deterioration. The Sandinistas refused to accept the kind of dependent relationship with the United States that had marked U.S.-Nicaraguan affairs for most of the twentieth century, and they cultivated connections to Cuba and the Soviet

Union. In addition, the Sandinistas postponed previously promised elections. They tightened restrictions on opposition activities and arrested many critics. And they encouraged leftist revolts in neighboring countries.

Carter administration officials tried to stem the deterioration in relations, but to no avail. When American ambassador Lawrence Pezzullo warned a minister of the Nicaraguan government that its support of foreign insurgencies couldn't help hurting relations with Washington, he was told that what Managua did was none of the Americans' affair. Pezzullo answered, referring to the recently appropriated aid: "Look, to be perfectly frank, I've spent ten months fighting for this goddamn money, and if that's your attitude I'll tell you to fuck off."[8]

Carter wasn't quite so blunt, but Reagan essentially was. To the conservatives of the Reagan administration, the Sandinistas' actions seemed sure signals that Nicaragua was slipping into the Soviet sphere, with consequences undoubtedly deleterious to the safety of the hemisphere. "The Sandinistas began trying to export their Marxist revolution to neighboring El Salvador and other countries in Central America," Reagan recalled. Any hints of good behavior were merely eyewash. "They proved themselves masters at propaganda, peddling an image of themselves in Europe and America as kindly men whose democratic reforms were being thwarted by the Great Colossus of the North—us."[9]

The administration responded in two ways: first by cutting off American aid, and second by devising a plan for covert operations against the Sandinista government. As it subsequently developed, the administration's covert plan involved supplies and training for an army of anti-Sandinista insurgents: the contras. Some of the contras were disaffected former supporters of the Nicaraguan revolution; others were out-of-work erstwhile members of Somoza's National Guard. More than a few had reputations for brutality and mercenary motives. Yet their checkered pedigree wouldn't prevent Reagan from calling them "the moral equivalent of the Founding Fathers." The contras would be based in Honduras, a country whose government had been friendly with Somoza and even friendlier with Washington.[10]

[8]Bob Woodward, *Veil* (New York, 1987), 114.
[9]Ronald Reagan, *An American Life* (New York, 1990), 300.
[10]*Weekly Compilation of Presidential Documents*, Mar. 11, 1985.

For the foreseeable future, the odds that the contras would over-throw the Sandinistas were nearly nil, but they could certainly make the Sandinista regime's life miserable. In the process, the Reagan administration hoped, the strains caused by the contras' efforts would spread disillusionment with the regime. The regime would weaken and would either modify its behavior or fall. Moreover, the contra war would diminish Managua's ability to export revolution to other parts of Central America, especially El Salvador, where a bloody civil war had broken out in 1980.

Things didn't develop quite according to plan. The pressure applied by the Reagan administration—pressure that came to include economic and political sanctions as well as the paramilitary efforts of the contras—did indeed add to Nicaragua's troubles. But during the early 1980s, the Sandinistas managed to keep dissatisfaction with the regime in check. To some extent, their success in doing so resulted from the fact that they retained a great deal of popular support for their educational, health, and other reforms. To some extent, it resulted from their active suppression of dissent. With passing time, the revolution shifted farther to the left, and early promises of civil liberties and democratic practices receded into the future.

Although the leftward shift of the Nicaraguan government confirmed the Reagan administration in its belief that the Sandinistas were basically Marxist-Leninists who had no respect for freedom or other values espoused by most Americans, the shift failed to convince certain influential members of Congress that Nicaragua posed a dire threat to fundamental American interests. Congressional critics of Reagan's Nicaragua policy felt uncomfortable funding the contras, whose unsavory antecedents and questionable practices reflected poorly on the United States. In 1982, the critics lined up behind an amendment sponsored by Democratic congressman Edward Boland of Massachusetts forbidding covert actions designed to overthrow the Nicaraguan government. The amendment passed, but because it included no provisions for enforcement, and because the Reagan administration contended for public consumption that the goal of the contra program was the interdiction of weapons shipments from the Sandinistas to the leftist rebels in El Salvador, the administration's anti-Sandinista offensive continued, much as before.

In fact, it intensified. Late in 1983, Reagan approved a C.I.A. plan to lay mines in Nicaragua's harbors, and during the next few months the plan was implemented. The purpose of the mining was to scare off foreign shippers and thereby increase the Sandinistas' already substantial economic woes. Realizing what they were up against, the Sandinistas would become more malleable.

The mining operation backfired. The mines damaged only a few ships and those not seriously, and harbor traffic continued about as usual. The injury to the Reagan administration's prestige was considerably greater. When the news of the mining operation leaked, the administration launched a damage-control operation, headed by William Casey. The C.I.A. director had a reputation as a hard man to corner, based largely on his habit of mumbling when he wanted to avoid giving a straight answer. But not entirely based on that: as David Stockman, Reagan's budget director remarked, "I figured he had to be smart. You didn't get where he'd been—S.E.C. [Securities and Exchange Commission] chairman, Wall Street tycoon—simply on bad elocution." In the case of the mining, Casey told an oversight board investigating the affair that the real question to be answered was: How did it leak? This prompted board member and noted lawyer Edward Bennett Williams to reply, in a combination of irritation and admiration: "You are a master of diversion. You are caught with a smoking gun in your hand, and you yell robbery." The congressional investigation showed Casey at his finest. While he apologized for any misbehavior the administration might have engaged in, he supplied administration supporters on the committee sufficient evidence to defend the covert approach. The highlight came when conservative Utah Republican Jake Garn denounced his colleagues for trying to handcuff the administration. "You're all assholes," Garn shouted. "You're all assholes—the whole Congress is full of assholes, all five hundred thirty-five members are assholes." To which committee member Daniel Patrick Moynihan responded, "Smile when you call me an asshole."[11]

For all his obfuscatory efforts, Casey couldn't keep Congress from passing additional legislation designed to collar the covert operators. The legislature approved a resolution condemning the mining, and Representative Boland introduced a new amendment further restricting administration activities in Nicaragua. The 1984 Boland amendment was worded so broadly as to prohibit the C.I.A., the Defense Department, "or any other agency or entity of the United States involved in intelligence activities" from expending

[11]David A. Stockman, *The Triumph of Politics* (New York, 1986), 49; Woodward, *Veil*, 383.

funds for the purpose "of supporting, directly or indirectly, military or paramilitary operations in Nicaragua by any nation, group, organization, movement or individual."[12]

Upon passage in October 1984, the Boland amendment appeared to signal an end to the Reagan administration's contra operation. But appearances deceived, and during the next two years administration go-getters would devise means to circumvent the law. In the meantime, though, the administration was content to give the impression that it was shifting to less belligerent tactics. Reagan understood that the month before the 1984 elections was no time for warmongering over a country few American voters cared much about. Reagan himself was a prohibitive favorite in the presidential election, but Republican candidates for the House and Senate were uncertain how long the president's coattails would be. They didn't want those coattails tattered in any scrapes in Central America. Moreover, Nicaraguan elections were also scheduled for November 1984, and while the anti-Sandinista hard-liners in Washington didn't trust the regime in Managua to allow a fair balloting, there seemed little reason to press the paramilitary option until the votes had been counted.

Finally, developments in El Salvador simultaneously contributed to a shift toward a less confrontational American policy toward Central America. Since the beginning of the Salvadoran civil war, the U.S. government had attempted to prevent El Salvador from going the way of Nicaragua. Many of the problems afflicting El Salvador were similar to those that had confronted Nicaragua during the last days of the Somoza regime. An uneven distribution of wealth and power alienated a large portion of the Salvadoran people from the government, while the Salvadoran military ruthlessly stifled dissent. A disparate assortment of rebels joined forces in the first half of 1980 as the Farabundo Martí National Liberation Front (F.M.L.N.) and plotted a "final offensive" to topple the military and the government.

Until late 1980, most Americans were only dimly aware of the turmoil in El Salvador. But in December of that year, Salvadoran security forces brutally murdered four American women, three of them Catholic nuns. The Carter administration, which to this point

---

[12]Pub. L. No. 98-473, 98 Stat. 1837, 1937 (Oct. 12, 1984), Continuing Resolution, Department of Defense Appropriations Act, Sec. 8066 (a).

had uneasily backed the government in San Salvador, responded to the killing by suspending American military aid.

The suspension didn't stick, however. Only weeks later, the F.M.L.N. proclaimed the beginning of its offensive. Carter, stinging from the charges that he lacked the spine to deal with radical threats to American interests, and aware that the incoming Reagan administration almost certainly would restore aid to the Salvadoran government, went ahead and did so himself. For good measure, he increased the weapons and supplies bound for San Salvador.

Reagan took the baton from Carter and ran even harder with it. The hawks in the new administration deemed El Salvador a domino in the communist quest for control of Central America. Alexander Haig described a four-stage Soviet-Cuban offensive. "First is the seizure of Nicaragua," Haig said. "Next is El Salvador, to be followed by Honduras and Guatemala." Referring to Soviet and Cuban assistance to the rebels in El Salvador, the State Department called that country "a textbook case of indirect armed aggression by Communist powers through Cuba."[13]

The external support for the Salvadoran insurgency did indeed exist, although the Reagan administration exaggerated its importance. And this external support provided the link between the administration's policies toward El Salvador and Nicaragua. "Our problem with El Salvador is external intervention in the internal affairs of a sovereign nation in this hemisphere, nothing more, nothing less," Haig declared. The secretary of state oversimplified matters; the Reagan administration almost certainly would have opposed even a strictly internal left-wing insurgency against the Salvadoran government. But the Soviet and Cuban assistance to the F.M.L.N. made the administration's opposition easier to justify, and the fact that some of the assistance was channeled through Nicaragua provided a handy rationale for the contra war against the Sandinistas.[14]

While the Reagan administration didn't deny that the Salvadoran government suffered from some deficiencies regarding human rights, the administration refused to accept that those deficiencies were grounds for letting the rebels win. Civil wars aren't tea parties, they explained. The Salvadoran military might be treating some of the country's citizens rather roughly, but as long as the Sal-

---

[13]Thomas Carothers, *In the Name of Democracy* (Berkeley, 1991), 13, 17.
[14]Ibid., 16.

vadoran government remained noncommunist, there was hope for reform. Should the F.M.L.N. take over, reform would be a lost cause.

In this strategy, American aid played a double role. It helped prevent a rebel victory, and it provided the United States some leverage in moving the Salvadoran military to straighten up. Such at least was the theory behind the Reagan administration's policy. In practice, however, the military caught on that Washington wasn't making human rights reform a priority, and the Salvadoran generals concentrated on suppressing the insurgency by whatever means appeared necessary. The death toll in El Salvador mounted appallingly, with thousands of civilians murdered by the security forces (and many by the rebels). Although Congress, in approving aid to El Salvador, required the president to ascertain that the Salvadoran government and military were achieving progress in respecting human rights, Reagan did so rather blithely. The president contended that most of the murders were the work either of rebels trying to make the government and the military look bad or of right-wing death squads that operated beyond the control of the government. The administration ignored much solid evidence that the members of the death squads were simply off-duty soldiers and officers—and not always off-duty.

The administration took encouragement in March 1984 when elections in El Salvador returned the relatively moderate José Napoleon Duarte to the presidency. The C.I.A. had contributed to Duarte's victory by providing covert campaign funds—reportedly between $1 million and $3 million. Officials at the American embassy in San Salvador didn't try to hide their support for Duarte. A few of the real ideologues in the Reagan administration favored the charismatic reactionary Roberto D'Aubuisson over Duarte, contending that D'Aubuisson would better be able to deal with the insurgency, but evidence linking D'Aubuisson to the death squads put off the administration as a whole.

When Duarte defeated D'Aubuisson, the administration claimed victory for its policy of continuing involvement in Salvadoran affairs. Some critics of the Reagan administration wondered how much control Duarte would be able to exert over the military, but Congress found the administration's reasoning sufficiently sound that in May 1984 it approved a large new package of economic and military aid. Duarte himself mollified critics of Reagan's confrontational approach by declaring in October 1984 that his government would commence negotiations with the rebels. This announcement didn't please some of the hawks in Washington, who thought negotiations were premature, but even they had to admit that it made the administration's life easier. With Congress in the process of approving the Boland amendment, and with the American elections at hand, anything that eased life for the administration regarding Central America was appreciated.

3. LEBANON'S DEADLY CHAOS

Related to the troubles the Reagan administration encountered in Central America—although related in a way that was secret at the time—were simultaneous difficulties in the Middle East. The Middle Eastern problem that had most vexed Jimmy Carter, namely the Iranian hostage affair, cleared itself up almost before Reagan finished swearing to uphold and defend the Constitution. On January 20, 1981, the hostage-takers released the fifty-two Americans, who were flown to West Germany and from there home. Some Reagan partisans attributed the timing of the release to the fear the new no-nonsense president struck in the Iranians. Skeptics suggested that the government in Teheran had decided that the hostages had served their purpose and that Iran would only be damaged by continued classification as an international outlaw. Out-and-out cynics thought they saw evidence of a clandestine deal between the Reagan camp—probably in the person of campaign manager and subsequently chief spook Casey—and Teheran, by which Teheran agreed to hold the hostages until Carter was defeated in the 1980 election and the Reagan people agreed to help Iran acquire spare parts for American weapons inherited from the shah. Iran sorely needed the spare parts following the outbreak of war with Iraq in September 1980. Among the evidence adduced by the cynics was a major resupply operation for Iran mounted from Israel shortly after Reagan's inauguration. Israeli ambassador Moshe Arens admitted later that in commencing this operation Israel had consulted with the U.S. government "at nearly the highest levels." The Reagan administration categorically denied any such deal with Teheran, but when subsequent similar denials fell afoul of incontrovertible facts (in the Iran-contra affair) the cynicism surfaced once more.[15]

[15]*New York Times*, Apr. 15, 1991.

If Reagan thought the early release of the hostages indicated smoother sailing for the United States in the Middle East, he was quickly disabused of the notion. The 1979 peace treaty between Israel and Egypt had failed to lead to any more-comprehensive pacts, contrary to the hopes of the signatories and the Carter administration. If anything, the Israel-Egypt treaty poisoned the well for further motion on the Arab-Israeli dispute. Confrontationalists among the Arabs decried the defection of Sadat from the anti-Israel front and vowed vengeance against all imitators. Their vows gained chilling credibility when Islamic zealots assassinated Sadat in 1981. Coming after a bloody assault on the Grand Mosque in Mecca, which was supposed to be under the protection of the comparatively moderate government of Saudi Arabia, Sadat's murder put the fear of Allah, or at least of those who claimed to be acting on His behalf, into would-be Arab peacemakers. Peacemakers predictably grew scarce among the Arabs.

This was a shame and a tragedy, for peacemakers were needed more than ever during the early 1980s. They were needed most in Lebanon, which still suffered from the same stresses that had triggered an American military intervention in 1958. The imbalance between the comparatively powerful and mostly conservative Christian minority and the comparatively powerless and often radical Muslim majority had grown worse in the intervening generation, largely because of the Muslims' greater fecundity. Complaints by other groups, notably the Druze, a sect of eclectic religious background, complicated the situation. Additional complications had followed the arrival of thousands of Palestinian guerrillas after an abortive uprising in Jordan in 1970. The Palestinians converted southern Lebanon into a base for operations against Israel. At the same time, they sided with the radical Muslims in Lebanese politics against the conservative Christians. The situation grew increasingly unstable until 1975, when Lebanon exploded into civil war. The main contestants were militia groups of, respectively, the radical Muslims and the conservative Christians. The Druze had an army and an agenda of their own.

Because Lebanon is small and sits in a volatile neighborhood, the troubles in that country soon splashed across its borders. Syria, reiterating a longstanding claim that Lebanon was rightfully part of a greater Syria, decided to intervene in the Lebanese war, basically to prevent a victory by the radical Lebanese Muslims and their allies from the Palestine Liberation Organization. Syrian president Asad didn't exactly embrace the cause of the Lebanese Christians, but he had no desire to see Lebanon fall under the control of the P.L.O., which seemed to want to provoke another war against Israel. Asad wasn't ready for such a war, not just yet. In 1976 he ordered thirteen thousand troops and hundreds of tanks into Lebanon.

Syria's entry into Lebanon set trigger fingers twitching in Israel. The Israelis feared that Syria would seize control of southern Lebanon as a base from which to attack northern Israel when Asad thought the time was ripe. The border region between Israel and Lebanon had been a lively (or rather, deadly) area for more than a decade, with the P.L.O. guerrillas lobbing mortar shells into Israel from Lebanon, and the Israeli army and air force staging reprisal raids. Israeli activities escalated significantly in 1978 when Israel's armed forces drove several miles into Lebanon, pushing the P.L.O. units north beyond the Litani River.

The Litani operation calmed the border for a time, but gradually the Palestinian guerrillas resumed their old ways. The Israeli government decided to seek a more permanent solution. In the spring of 1982, Israel launched Operation Peace for Galilee, whose ostensible purpose was to establish a guerrilla-free zone in southern Lebanon. But as Israeli forces poured into Lebanon and advanced far past the southern border region, foreign observers—and many Israelis—suspected that this latest operation had larger objectives, perhaps including the annihilation of the P.L.O. in Lebanon and the expulsion of the Syrians.

The Reagan administration required some time to make up its mind regarding the significance of the Israeli invasion of Lebanon. Administration hawks such as Alexander Haig were quite content for Israel to smash the P.L.O. and the Syrians. Haig saw the contest for Lebanon as a proxy version of the Cold War, with American client Israel representing Washington and Soviet client Syria standing in for Moscow. (The P.L.O. didn't fit so neatly into the picture but was closer to Moscow than to Washington.) An Israeli success would redound to the prestige of the United States, while an Israeli failure would tarnish America's reputation. The Reagan administration, Haig argued, ought to assist the Israelis, or at least do nothing to hinder them.

Opposing Haig were defense secretary Weinberger and Vice President George Bush. Weinberger and Bush conceded that the conflict in Lebanon could have important consequences for the global contest between the United States and the Soviet Union, but they placed greater emphasis on the regional ramifications. Taking much the same line as the Nixon administration had during the October War of 1973, Weinberger and Bush argued that an overwhelming Israeli success in Lebanon would set the chances for peace in the area back many years. And absent peace, the Soviets would continue to be tempted to meddle in the Middle East.

Reagan wavered between these opposing views. At first he seemed to support the Israeli offensive. While other Western leaders were condemning Israel's action, the American president kept silent. Because American weapons were playing a major role in the Israeli offensive, Reagan's silence seemed to imply approval. The implication grew stronger when the administration vetoed a United Nations resolution calling for sanctions against Israel.

But as the larger extent of Israeli ambitions became evident, Reagan began to reconsider the apparent approval his silence conveyed. The Israelis swept southern Lebanon clear of the P.L.O. and headed northward to Beirut. Along the way, they beat up on Syrian units, throwing some back into the Bekaa Valley and cornering others in the Lebanese capital. The Israeli air force destroyed dozens of Syrian planes, suffering almost no losses itself.

The hawks in the Reagan administration cheered the Israelis on. Haig called the impending Israeli victory a "great opportunity for peace." Going beyond his arguments about Israel's acting in America's stead, the secretary of state contended that conditions in Lebanon had lately reached such chaos that balance among the warring parties was impossible. Peace would have to be imposed from outside. The Israelis had the will and capacity to do so; Washington should give them the green light.[16]

The Middle East moderates in the administration continued to dispute Haig's reasoning. Weinberger and Bush pointed out that the United States was already incurring blame for the deaths and devastation the Israelis were inflicting on Lebanon. The higher the death toll and the greater the devastation, the more blame would be pinned on Washington. The Israelis must be made to halt.

At this stage, Reagan swung to the side of Weinberger and Bush, precipitating Haig's resignation. Reagan wrote to Menachem Begin

[16]Alexander M. Haig Jr., *Caveat* (New York, 1984), 342.

saying that the prime minister must pull back Israel's troops. When Begin visited Washington at the end of June, the president reemphasized his point. The meeting—the second between the two leaders—didn't go easily. "When we shook hands, it was still 'Menachem' and 'Ron,' but our meeting had none of the glow of our previous meeting," Reagan recalled. "With only our ambassadors present, Begin and I spent almost an hour going head to head."[17]

Grudgingly, Begin allowed himself to be persuaded, but slowly enough to let Israel's soldiers punish the P.L.O. some more. American negotiator Philip Habib mediated a deal whereby the Israelis would stop shooting long enough for the P.L.O. fighters to withdraw from Beirut. Motivating the Israeli side, in addition to the pressure from Washington, was the fact that the Israeli public was registering reservations about a house-to-house battle that would drench the Lebanese capital in blood, mostly Palestinian but much Israeli as well. Motivating the P.L.O. was the belief of its leaders that they had made their point and that wisdom now consisted in living to fight another day. Reassuring both sides was an American promise of a peacekeeping contingent to help monitor the evacuation.

The evacuation itself went smoothly enough. By mid-September more than eight thousand P.L.O. soldiers had left Beirut for Algeria, Tunisia, and other radical parts of the Arab world. Several thousand Syrian troops took advantage of the lull in fighting to head home to Syria. Within weeks the American peacekeepers went back to their ships, and nearly everyone concerned breathed a sigh of relief. The Reagan administration was particularly pleased that the operation had debunked the expressed worries of many critics that the United States was entering a Vietnam-like quagmire.

The relief proved premature. In late September an assassin murdered the Christian president of Lebanon, Bashir Gemayel. Christian militiamen retaliated by entering two Palestinian refugee camps near Beirut and massacring some eight hundred women, children, old people, and anyone else they could lay hands on. Israeli troops in the area stood by and let the killing proceed.

The massacres at the Sabra and Shatila camps immediately brought calls for a return of the American peacekeepers. The Palestinian civilians in Lebanon hadn't wanted the P.L.O. guerrillas to leave, for without the guerrillas the civilians felt defenseless—not only against Israel's army but also against their Arab enemies. The massacres showed these fears to be well founded. The Reagan administration, having dodged charges from one direction that it was acting rashly in sending troops into Lebanon, now confronted complaints that it had acted hastily in pulling the troops out. To counter these latter complaints, the president agreed to send several hundred marines back to Beirut.

What they were to do there, though, wasn't entirely clear. They might be able to forestall further score-settling of the kind that had killed the eight hundred Palestinians, but what else they would do was an open question.

Part of the answer was that they might get shot at. The U.S. marines entered Lebanon at the request of the Lebanese government, a circumstance that almost automatically placed them on the hit list of the numerous groups opposing the government. The injection of the troops put other Americans in the country at risk also.

The hitting started relatively gently. Uncertain what the Americans were up to, the insurgents confined themselves to occasional sniper rounds. Yet gradually things got hotter. Rebel fire against the American marines intensified, and then in April 1983 a Shiite Muslim suicide bomber blasted the American embassy in Beirut. Seventeen Americans and twenty-three other persons died in the attack.

The tragedy at the embassy provoked new criticism of the Reagan administration's Lebanon policy. The critics demanded to know just what the American soldiers—and, for that matter, American diplomats and other officials—were trying to accomplish in that war-crazed country. As usual, the criticism reflected both honest differences and partisan point-scoring. Democrats unhappy with Reagan for assorted reasons, some having to do with foreign affairs and some not, were happy to suggest again that the administration was leading the United States into another Vietnam. The administration assured the American people that Lebanon was no Vietnam.

The critics seemed to have the better of the argument during the summer and early autumn of 1983. Rebel forces near Beirut increasingly targeted the Americans, and while the administration didn't really want to get more deeply involved in the fighting, neither did it wish to see American soldiers in a position where they weren't allowed to defend themselves. Such might be fatally unfair to the soliders. It could also be tremendously embarrassing to the administration, many of whose supporters believed that the American debacle in Vietnam had resulted from the American military's having to fight the war there hamstrung by political concerns.

Under strong pressure from the Pentagon, the president authorized retaliation against the Lebanese insurgents. American jets flew reconnaissance missions over rebel strongholds, which American warships just off the coast proceeded to bombard. Firefights between the marines and the rebels grew more intense than ever. By late September the United States seemed on its way to becoming a full-fledged belligerent in the Lebanese war.

The escalating American activity in Lebanon prompted two significant responses—one from people who wished the United States well and the other from people who didn't. The benign response was a congressional resolution requiring the president to accept an eighteen-month time limit on the deployment of U.S. troops in Lebanon. Reagan didn't like the idea of such a limit, believing that it infringed on his prerogatives as commander-in-chief. But to resist it too strenuously would give the distinct impression that Lebanon might indeed become the morass the administration's critics were calling it. So Reagan accepted the measure under protest.

The other response—the malign one—was more dramatic and, as matters turned out, more effective in limiting the American stay in Lebanon. On October 23 another Shiite terrorist drove a truck packed with explosives into the U.S. marine encampment at the Beirut airport. When the terrorist detonated his rolling bomb, the explosion killed 241 American marines and 58 French soldiers.

If the administration had previously developed a stronger case for the American presence in Lebanon, Americans might have reacted to this latest tragedy the way Americans of an earlier generation had reacted to the bombing of Pearl Harbor. But most Americans couldn't make much sense out of the turmoil in Lebanon, and few could see why American soldiers ought to get themselves killed there. For a brief moment the administration attempted to act as steadfast as ever, contending that terrorists would not run the United States out of Lebanon. But with public support for the American presence in Lebanon dwindling rapidly, the administration announced early in 1984 that it would "redeploy" the American marines from Beirut to ships offshore. Reagan put the best face he could on the situation. "We're not bugging out," he declared. "We're just going to a little more defensible position."[18]

The lesson of Reagan's first term should have been that while simplicity sells, it doesn't buy. Reagan's world was a world of good and evil, of democratic freedom and communist slavery, of American rectitude and Soviet subversion. The real world was different. The real world was the world of suicide bombers in Lebanon, of Jonas Savimbis and Khmer Rouge genocides, of the C.I.A. mining harbors in Nicaragua, of atrocities by American clients in El Salvador, of Weinberger's six reasons not to use all his shiny new weapons.

But most Americans didn't find the discrepancy between the world according to Reagan and the world according to reality particularly distressing. The president remained immensely popular, and so, apparently, did his message that the world was still the way Americans had gotten used to it in the years just after 1945. Given their choice, most Americans would have been happy to have it stay that way.

[18]*American Foreign Policy 1984*, 581.

CHAPTER 4

The Old Order Collapses: 1985–1989

The Reaganist worldview took a battering during the second half of the 1980s. The world grew only more complicated, and the postwar structure of international affairs disintegrated. The most spectacular display of disintegration occurred in Eastern Europe, where Mikhail Gorbachev oversaw the dissolution of the Soviet Union's foreign empire. Though long hoped for in the rhetoric of American leaders, the reality of the collapse of the European order forced a reconsideration of American interests and objectives. For forty years Americans hadn't really had to worry about what happened in Eastern Europe; that was Moscow's sphere. Despite the obnoxious aspects of Soviet rule, it had the virtue of maintaining order. How order would be maintained now, no one could say. To cite only the most worrisome question: Who would keep the Germans in line once they reunited?

The Middle East was even more tumultuous than usual. The biggest war of the region's twentieth-century history was embroiling Iran and Iraq, and it enmeshed the United States as well. The Reagan administration got tangled up selling arms to Iran, in defiance of American law and its own public policy. The goal was to free American hostages held in Lebanon (and, in an additional complicating twist, to generate profits earmarked for the Nicaraguan contras); the result was to thoroughly compromise the administration's reputation and much of its effectiveness. As if this wasn't enough, the administration also got mixed up in the Iran-Iraq war on the side of Iraq.

Quieter but arguably more portentous were developments in the world economy. The most obvious was the emergence of Japan as an economic superpower. Exactly what this meant was hard to tell. Japanese companies and individuals bought up American corporations, American real estate, and American treasury bonds. But Japanese consumers didn't buy much in the way of American exports—or not nearly as much as American consumers bought in the way of Japanese exports. Many analysts predicted that a chronic trade imbalance between the United States and Japan would result in a sapping of Americans' standard of living, as economic power drifted west across the Pacific. Worrying types forecast a breakdown of the cooperation that had typified U.S.-Japanese relations since 1945. A few genuine alarmists looked for a resumption of the rivalry that had typified Tokyo's dealings with Washington for several decades before the onset of the Cold War.

1. RUSSIA'S FIRST REVOLUTIONARY SINCE LENIN

Two months after Reagan was sworn in for the second time as U.S. president, Mikhail Gorbachev took up the reins of power in Moscow. The leadership in the Soviet Union had been in disarray since the death of Leonid Brezhnev in 1982. Yuri Andropov, Brezhnev's immediate successor as Communist party general secretary, lasted less than two years in the job before dying. Andropov's successor, Konstantin Chernenko, survived less than one year. After Chernenko, the Politburo looked for a younger man and found Gorbachev, who at fifty-five was a mere stripling by Kremlin standards.

Perhaps because of youthful impatience, Gorbachev quickly set about attempting major changes in the affairs of the Soviet Union. He first jolted Soviet society by launching an anti-alcohol campaign, sharply raising the price of vodka and other beverages with which overburdened Soviet citizens regularly eased their pain. He went on to denounce the bureaucracy for corruption and obstructionism. He stayed the hands of the Kremlin's censors and encouraged citizens to point out deficiencies in the government. He released political prisoners from jail and labor camps. He called for the injection of democratic practices into the Soviet political system. He advocated economic reforms that would break the stifling grip of government upon the energies of the Soviet people and thereby move the Soviet Union in the direction of a market economy.

Like any clever reformer, Gorbachev had catchy names for his reforms. *Glasnost* (openness) referred to efforts to shine the light of public scrutiny and criticism into the workings of the Soviet system. *Perestroika* (restructuring) referred to attempts to retool the Soviet political economy. Of the two, perestroika was the more fundamental, while glasnost was chiefly a means to perestroika's end. Gorbachev recognized that the Soviet Union was like a weight lifter afflicted with arthritis. If not forced to exert itself, it could still look impressive, but it had lost the suppleness and strength of youth, and its future promised only progressive paralysis. The Soviet malady was partly the result of the lack of incentives provided by the centralized, government-directed economy, and partly the result of the rigidity and corruption that commonly characterize regimes unaccountable to the people they rule. Gorbachev hoped to revitalize the Soviet Union by revamping Soviet politics and the Soviet economy.

Gorbachev's efforts elicited great support and great opposition. Support came from those who agreed that much was wrong with the Soviet system and needed to be changed. Such persons rallied to Gorbachev timidly at first, not knowing how firmly committed he really was to glasnost or whether he would survive politically. There had been thaws in the police-state repression in the past, but they had usually been followed by hard winters in Siberian labor camps for those who tried to take advantage of the warmth. But now, as people spoke and wrote their minds and didn't hear that midnight rifle butt against the door, the trickle of free discussion became a freshet and then a torrent. Soon almost nothing was sacred and above reproach anymore.

Which was precisely what those who opposed Gorbachev's reforms objected to. The opposition included people who had benefited materially from the status quo—Communist party functionaries, government bureaucrats, high-ranking military officers—as well as some who simply feared the uncertainty of change. Gorbachev had intended to reform the Soviet system, but his reforms turned into a veritable revolution, and revolutions frighten people. Many people in the Soviet Union (as in other countries) thought that national leaders should be treated with respect and not be subjected to criticism by just anyone with access to a microphone or a photocopy machine. Such people thought glasnost was getting out of control. Similarly, many in the Soviet Union valued the economic and psychological security of socialism and weren't enthusiastic about perestroika's push toward capitalism, with such attendant capitalist insecurities as wage cuts and unemployment.

During the latter half of the 1980s, the battle raged between the supporters of reform and the opponents. Glasnost proceeded more rapidly than perestroika, proving principally that razing old structures is easier than erecting new ones. In time, Gorbachev became almost incidental to the forces of change he had unleashed. Many of his erstwhile supporters started to think he wasn't moving fast enough in the direction of change, while most of his opponents still thought he was moving too fast. By 1989 he gave the impression of a man trying to navigate a canoe on a swift-flowing river filled with large and constantly colliding chunks of ice. For all his undeniable skills with a paddle, it seemed likely that the current and ice would prove too much for him.

2. LEARNING TO TAKE YES FOR AN ANSWER

Whatever the reaction within the Soviet Union to Gorbachev's reforms, governments and people in the Western democratic countries generally supported them enthusiastically. Some American skeptics initially had wondered whether glasnost and perestroika were merely smoke screens for more of the same in Soviet politics, with the Communist party still intending to hold tightly to the levers of authority. Others perceived Gorbachev's reforms as real, yet worried that a reinvigorated Soviet Union might pose an increased threat to the United States precisely on account of its reinvigoration. But as the changes in the Soviet Union gained momentum, most Americans saw Gorbachev as honestly leading his country toward political liberalization and a market economy, and considered the move praiseworthy.

George Shultz was an early convert to the view that Gorbachev was the genuine article. "He performs like a person who has been in charge for a while, not like a person who is just taking charge," the secretary of state commented after meeting Gorbachev at Chernenko's funeral. "A person who just got there simply cannot have that much command of information and self-confidence." In a conversation with Canadian prime minister Brian Mulroney, also at the funeral, Shultz was asked when he thought important changes in the Soviet system might commence. He answered in a word: "Today."[1]

[1]Don Oberdorfer, *The Turn* (New York, 1991), 109–11.

Gorbachev valued the American support, and not only because people undertaking difficult tasks appreciate encouragement. A major component of his program was a planned reduction in spending on the Soviet military, which for years had claimed a heavy portion of the Soviet Union's economic output. At the Chernenko funeral the new general secretary proclaimed to Shultz and Vice President Bush that ending the arms race was imperative. Gorbachev explained that Soviet negotiators were preparing "very seriously" for upcoming arms talks in Geneva, and he hoped their American counterparts were too. Gorbachev expressed particular concern about the Reagan administration's desire, first professed in 1983 with the unveiling of the "strategic defense initiative," to project the weapons race into outer space. He warned Bush and Shultz that pursuing such new technologies could set in motion "irreversible and uncontrollable processes." He said he understood that certain people in the United States supported a continued arms race in the belief that it would wear the Soviet Union down economically. This was "a pipedream, nothing but adventurism," he said.[2]

Maybe it was, and maybe it wasn't. But an expensive extension of the arms race beyond the stratosphere might well jeopardize Gorbachev's chances of reforming the Soviet system, and he did everything he could to prevent it. His opposition to space-based weapons was part of a larger arms-control offensive. Since the demise of detente at the beginning of the decade, arms control between the superpowers had been primarily an exercise in rhetoric. Candidate Reagan had repeatedly criticized the SALT II treaty as "fatally flawed," and the pact languished unratified—although after election he consented, somewhat contradictorily, to abide informally by SALT II's provisions. The Republican president was committed to expanding and updating America's military forces, and he had no desire to handcuff himself by substantial arms-control measures.

Yet politics—domestic and international—required the administration at least to nod in the direction of restraining the arms race, and consequently it proposed what came to be called the "zero option" for intermediate nuclear forces (I.N.F.) in Europe. Following the deployment of a new generation of Soviet missiles, the SS-20s, in the western part of the Soviet Union, the Reagan administration laid plans to replace American intermediate missiles in Western Europe

---

[2]George P. Shultz, *Turmoil and Triumph* (New York, 1993), 530.

with newer and more powerful models, specifically Pershing II ballistic missiles and Tomahawk cruise missiles. But enough pro-detente sentiment lingered in Europe to render the American deployment politically delicate for the governments of the host NATO countries. In order to provide political cover for those governments, as well as to shield itself from charges by Democrats and others in the United States that it desired only to build weapons rather than control them, the Reagan administration offered to forgo the deployment of the new Pershings and Tomahawks if the Soviets would dismantle their SS-20s. The result would be no intermediate missiles on either side. Hence the label "zero option."

Moscow at first refused to take the American proposal seriously, which didn't surprise anyone. The American offer required the Soviet Union to remove missiles that were already in place in exchange for an American promise not to deploy missiles. Considering the touchy situation in the NATO countries, where anti-Pershing and anti-American demonstrations were a regular feature of political life, the new American missiles might well never be deployed at all. In essence, therefore, the Kremlin was being asked to give up real missiles in exchange for Washington's giving up hypothetical missiles. It seemed a bad deal for the Soviets, and they said so.

During the next few years, however, calculations changed. Despite the demonstrations in Britain, West Germany, and elsewhere, the U.S. missiles were gradually deployed. Consequently the zero option now would entail trading real American missiles for the Soviet missiles. Moreover, the American missiles were more threatening to the Soviet Union than the Soviet missiles were to the United States, as Soviet negotiators endlessly pointed out, because the Pershings and Tomahawks could hit targets inside the Soviet Union, while the SS-20s could not hit the United States. Indeed, with a mere eight-minute flight time, the Pershings could decapitate Moscow's command structure before the Kremlin knew there was a war on. The Tomahawks were slower but flew beneath radar and were almost equally frightening.

But the same considerations that made the zero option increasingly attractive to the Soviet leaders made it less attractive to the Reagan administration. As Gorbachev, in keeping with his desire to curtail Soviet defense spending, indicated interest in an I.N.F. treaty, the hard-liners in Washington attempted to up the ante. They argued that since Gorbachev was in a compromising mood, the Reagan administration should keep pushing him to see how far he would bend.

Yet other factors besides Gorbachev's desire to trim outlays on arms added to the momentum for a treaty. By the beginning of Reagan's second term, popular enthusiasm for lavishing money on the Pentagon was starting to thin. The federal deficit was mounting, and the big defense budget was a major contributor. Besides, Gorbachev didn't make a very convincing villain. With the Soviet Union evidently growing less dangerous by the day, increasing numbers of Americans thought the time had come for serious arms control.

Ronald Reagan eventually reached the same conclusion. To a certain extent, he was motivated by the feeling that affects all second-term presidents: a desire to accomplish something for historians to write about. Though proud of his military buildup, he wanted to be remembered as a man of peace. To a certain extent, Reagan was motivated by his favorable impression of Gorbachev. Just weeks after assuming power, Gorbachev had written to Reagan affirming his intention to "act vigorously" to improve U.S.-Soviet relations. In the same letter, he accepted Reagan's suggestion of a personal meeting. Where previous summits had commonly been for the purpose of signing prenegotiated agreements, Gorbachev didn't want to wait that long. "The main thing," the general secretary said, "is that it should be a meeting to search for mutual understanding on the basis of equality and account of legitimate interests of each other." Reagan responded positively to Gorbachev's letter. "I believe that new opportunities are now opening up in U.S.-Soviet relations," the president replied. "We must take advantage of them."[3]

This exchange set in motion the most productive personal relationship between any pair of U.S. and Soviet leaders in the history of the two countries. The two men met seven times between 1985 and the end of 1988: in the United States, in the Soviet Union, and in various neutral countries. Although they discussed a spectrum of topics during their meetings, from East-West trade to Third World politics, the sessions centered on arms control.

The most memorable meeting took place in Reykjavik, Iceland, in October 1986. During the previous year, the United States and the Soviet Union had swapped several proposals for reducing nuclear arsenals. Each side had attempted to cast itself as the true advocate

[3] Ronald Reagan, *An American Life* (New York, 1990), 614–15.

of arms control. Some genuine progress had been made toward an
I.N.F. treaty, not least because of the departure from the Reagan administration of the treaty's most adamant opponents, but in other
areas the two sides had basically talked past each other. Reagan and
Gorbachev went to Reykjavik determined to confront the issues
head-on.

It didn't take them long to agree to an I.N.F. accord along the
lines of the zero option. Gorbachev then expressed general support
for a proposal by Reagan to eliminate long-range missiles as well.
Gorbachev even went the president one better by suggesting the
elimination not merely of nuclear missiles but of all nuclear
weapons. Reagan responded with enthusiasm. For years the president had dreamed of ridding the world of the danger of nuclear war,
and now that dream seemed to be approaching reality. "It was a historic moment," remarked Reagan's chief of staff, Donald Regan.
"The two leaders had brought the world to one of its great turning
points."[4]

But then, as Reagan described the situation afterward, Gorbachev "threw the curve." The Soviet leader demanded that the
United States give up its space-defense program. Basic research
might continue, but there could be no testing or deployment of the
new technologies outside the laboratory.[5]

Reagan wouldn't bite. For all his ignorance on nuclear issues,
the president knew enough to detest the policy of "mutual assured
destruction" (MAD) which kept the peace by guaranteeing the re-
ciprocal annihilation of the superpowers in the event of war. And
consequently he was enchanted by the idea of a space-based defense
against nuclear missiles. It didn't hurt that the star wars scheme allowed the Republicans to reclaim the moral high ground from the
Democrats and others who held to MAD. As administration official
Kenneth Adelman said, "How ironic it is that liberals, who pride
themselves on their moral motives, advocate such a bloodcurdling
approach, namely that all is well as long as we can launch enough
missiles to kill a hundred million or so Soviets."[6]

Thus Reagan wasn't about to give up space defenses. He told
Gorbachev that the envisioned system threatened no one, and he

[4]Donald T. Regan, *For the Record* (New York, 1988), 391.
[5]Oberdorfer, *The Turn*, 195.
[6]Lou Cannon, *President Reagan* (New York, 1991), 322.

They seem agreeable here, but they couldn't
quite cut the deal: Ronald Reagan and Mikhail
Gorbachev at Reykjavik.
Reagan Library.

said that it would be needed as protection against third countries
even if the superpowers eliminated their nuclear arsenals.

When the president refused to reconsider, the grand schemes for
banishing nuclear weapons evaporated into the Iceland air. Reagan
left Reykjavik disappointed and upset. Gorbachev appeared equally
agitated.

Yet the disappointment and agitation soon passed. Although
Reagan and Gorbachev hadn't dismantled the entire nuclear arsenals of the two countries, they had made possible the elimination of
a large class of intermediate missiles. American and Soviet negotiators required another year after the Reykjavik summit to finalize the

details of verification and other technical matters, but in December 1987 Reagan and Gorbachev exchanged signatures on the completed I.N.F. treaty. Ratification followed within months, and the most ambitious arms-reduction pact of the Cold War to date soon took effect.

3. FIGHTING BOMBS WITH BOMBS

The I.N.F. treaty represented an attempt by the Reagan administration to reduce the risk of violence on a massive, nuclear scale. At the same time that it was negotiating the I.N.F. treaty, the administration was pursuing a different strategy for dealing with violence on another level.

The problem of international terrorism had only gotten worse since the American hostages had been released by Iran in 1981. Though the Reagan administration still worried about Iran's sponsorship of terrorist activities, for a time during the 1980s the country most often associated in American thinking with terrorism was Libya. In the 1950s and 1960s, the Libyan government of King Idris had cooperated with the United States, to the extent of allowing the Americans to operate a large air base not far from Tripoli. In 1969, however, a coup brought to power a new regime that started out vociferously anti-American and became violently so. The leader of the new regime, Muammar al-Qaddafi, evicted the Americans from the Wheelus base and raised the banner of radical revolution. The most obvious and consistent target of Qaddafi's excoriations was Israel, but Israel was also the most mundane, in that even conservative Arab governments denounced the Zionists with every second breath. Qaddafi distinguished himself by taking on several fellow Arab leaders as well. He scored the governments of Egypt, Jordan, Morocco, and Tunisia, sometimes venturing beyond rhetorical aggression to more substantial modes. He furnished logistical support to insurgents conspiring to overthrow the conservative regimes, and he embraced the concept of terrorism as a legitimate weapon of the dispossessed against the powerful.

Qaddafi's first widely publicized substantive venture into terrorism was the provision of after-the-fact sanctuary to several Palestinians of the Black September movement who kidnapped and then killed eleven Israeli athletes at the 1972 Munich Olympic Games. His involvement in subsequent terrorist incidents was harder to document, but the evidence was sufficient to convince most Western governments that terrorism formed an integral part of Qaddafi's approach to the world. Qaddafi himself sometimes openly admitted as much. Although the Libyan government endorsed various United Nations proclamations condemning terrorism, Qaddafi reserved the right to define what he meant by the word. He didn't include in his definition certain efforts by small countries to protect themselves against the great powers—which, he insisted, hypocritically practiced terrorism on a daily basis. "Foreign bases, nuclear weapons, starvation, economic warfare, naval fleets"—all these, he claimed, were "acts of terrorism." Speaking specifically of actions like those of the Black September terrorists, Qaddafi demanded, "Why do Americans forget that the Palestinians have been expelled from their homeland and that the U.S. is helping the occupier keep hold of the land of the Palestinians? But when a Palestinian hijacks a plane to express his despair, the U.S. shakes the world by saying that this is terrorism and an end should be put to it."[7]

The United States shook the world on the subject of terrorism only halfheartedly before the 1980s. Jimmy Carter identified Libya as a sponsor of international terrorism, but did little to punish Qaddafi. Carter had more than enough trouble with Iran and didn't feel like adding Libya to his list of headaches.

Ronald Reagan adopted a different approach. The Republican president augmented American aid to governments under attack by Qaddafi's propaganda and subversion and, more to the point, mounted a counteroffensive against the Libyan leader. The C.I.A. outfitted and trained a small army of anti-Qaddafi Libyan exiles. Whether this band ever got so far as to formulate specific plans for ousting Qaddafi is unclear, but at the least its existence and efforts reminded him that Washington was watching. Qaddafi reacted defiantly. "We are capable of exporting terrorism to the heart of America," he declared. "We are also capable of physical liquidation, destruction, and arson inside America." Americans had inflicted terrorism on Libya, he reiterated. "We will respond likewise." For good measure he added, "We are always wronged; therefore we have the right to fight Zionism, we have the right to fight America, and we have the right to export terrorism to them because they have done everything to us."[8]

[7]Mahmoud G. El-Warfally, *Imagery and Ideology in U.S. Policy toward Libya, 1969–1982* (Pittsburgh, 1988), 72.
[8]Brian L. Davis, *Qaddafi, Terrorism, and the Origins of the U.S. Attack on Libya* (New York, 1990), 66, 185.

From the perspective of the Reagan administration, Qaddafi was just asking for trouble with statements like these, and the administration was glad to oblige. On two occasions during the 1980s, the United States took direct military action against Qaddafi. The first and less destructive blow fell on Libya in 1981, when U.S. warplanes shot down two Libyan MiGs over the Gulf of Sidra. Qaddafi claimed the gulf as Libya's own, but Washington (and most other maritime nations) judged it to be part of international waters. When the Libyan fighters approached the American planes in a threatening manner, the American pilots rocketed them.

The larger incident occurred in 1986. The previous few years had witnessed an upsurge of terrorism. After the bombings of the American embassy in Lebanon and the U.S. marine barracks at the Beirut airport, terrorists had hijacked planes, including an American T.W.A. airliner, and gone on shooting rampages at the Rome and Vienna airports. Reagan responded in January 1986 by declaring a national emergency with respect to Libya. He slapped an embargo on trade with Libya and froze Libyan assets in the United States. The president justified these measures by calling the Rome and Vienna massacres "the latest in a series of atrocities which have shocked the conscience of the world." He went on to say, "Qaddafi's longstanding involvement in terrorism is well documented, and there's irrefutable evidence of his role in these attacks." (Questioned afterward on the subject, Reagan declined to reveal the precise nature of the evidence.) He called for Qaddafi to be treated as "a pariah in the world community." Referring to the economic sanctions he had just imposed, Reagan concluded, "If these steps do not end Qaddafi's terrorism, I promise you that further steps will be taken."[9]

The further steps weren't long in coming. Qaddafi continued to hurl defiance at Washington, so Reagan ordered the Sixth Fleet to undertake maneuvers close to Libya's coast in the Gulf of Sidra. The administration made no secret of its desire to provoke Qaddafi into some rash action. An administration official who requested anonymity told a reporter, "Of course we're aching for a go at Qaddafi." Another official promised, "If he sticks his head up, we'll clobber him. We're looking for an excuse."[10]

Qaddafi played into Washington's hands when he directed Libya's shore batteries to fire on the American vessels. The com-

[9]*American Foreign Policy: Current Documents 1986*, 446–47.
[10]Davis, *Qaddafi, Terrorism, and the Origins of the U.S. Attack on Libya*, 104.

mander of the Sixth Fleet ordered reprisals against Libyan targets, and within hours U.S. planes destroyed Libyan radar installations and sank or crippled several Libyan patrol boats, with substantial casualties to the crews manning them. The Reagan administration expressed satisfaction with the results of the raids, but indicated a desire for more. An administration spokesman promised, "The next act of terrorism will bring the hammer down."[11]

The next act took place in West Berlin at the beginning of April. A bomb exploded in a crowded nightclub, killing two American servicemen and injuring hundreds of other people. The administration quickly concluded that Qaddafi was responsible. "Our evidence is direct," the president said. "It is precise. It is irrefutable."[12]

Subsequent reports suggested that the situation might have been more complicated than Reagan indicated, in particular that Syria's Asad may have had more to do with the Berlin bombing than Qaddafi. But Reagan was in no mood to debate rules of evidence. Convinced that Qaddafi deserved punishment for other acts of terrorism, even if not for this one, the president ordered American warplanes to deliver the promised hammer blow. On April 15, American bombers based in Britain joined planes from American aircraft carriers in the Mediterranean for an attack against Libyan targets in Tripoli and Benghazi. One of those targets may have been Qaddafi himself, although the administration refused to confirm that it was trying specifically to kill him. (One reason for the refusal to confirm may have been the post-Watergate reform that outlawed assassination of foreign leaders.) While the American bombs failed to find Qaddafi, they killed dozens of other Libyans, including a young girl Qaddafi claimed as his daughter. (Skeptics on the subject of Qaddafi suggested posthumous adoption.) Damage to Libyan facilities was severe.

The American attack on Libya precipitated protests within the United States and around the world. The protesters argued that Reagan, in launching an attack on a country with which the United States was not at war, was no better than Qaddafi. British prime minister Margaret Thatcher stood by Reagan, but the governments of other allies put some distance between themselves and Washington. France had wanted so little to do with the attack that it rejected

---

[11]*Newsweek*, April 7, 1986.
[12]*Weekly Compilation of Presidential Documents*, April 21, 1986.

American requests for the attacking U.S. planes from Britain to fly over French territory on the way to Libya. Many of the critics predicted that the American raid against Libya would cause a new round of terrorist actions.

On this point the critics were right, at least in the short term. Soon after the Libyan raid, unidentified gunmen seriously wounded an American diplomat in Sudan. Another American official was shot in Yemen. Two Libyans armed with grenades were arrested near a U.S. officers' club in Turkey. An American kidnapped in Beirut was murdered and the body dumped on the street. The American embassy in Indonesia came under rocket fire.

Qaddafi applauded the attackers and all who assaulted Americans and American property and institutions. The Libyan government radio station called Reagan a "mad terrorist" and declared, "He who kills an American enters heaven. He who slaughters an American creates a new glory for the Arab nation with blood."[13]

In the longer term, however, the situation quieted down and terrorist activity diminished. Reagan's partisans predictably asserted that the president's bold actions had chastened Qaddafi. There may have been some truth to such assertions, although much of the reduction in terrorism probably resulted from heightened vigilance by numerous governments around the world. Security at airports and other sensitive spots was tightened up, making the terrorists' work harder. West European governments deported suspicious-looking foreigners, especially those of Middle Eastern background. Civil libertarians and advocates of equal treatment for Arabs complained, but the governments cited national security. In some cases, it was unclear whether the governments were worried more about Qaddafi or about Reagan. They didn't want the Libyan leader to get away with further violence, but neither did they want the U.S. president to find another excuse for making war against Libya.

4. ARMS FOR THE AYATOLLAH, DOLLARS FOR THE CONTRAS

One of the reasons Reagan went after Qaddafi was that Libya made such an easy target. Other sponsors of Middle Eastern terrorism

---

[13]Davis, *Qaddafi, Terrorism, and the Origins of the U.S. Attack on Libya*, 189.

were harder to hit without incurring unacceptable risks. Iran's Khomeini continued to call anathemas down on the head of the "Great Satan" of the West, and the ayatollah's followers attempted to prove their devotion to the Islamic revolution by assaulting Americans in the Middle East. For years before the outbreak of the civil war in Lebanon, that country had been the cosmopolitan cross-roads of the region, and many Americans and other foreign nationals made Beirut their home and workplace. Some of these expatriates left when the fighting started, but others hoped for a return of peace and stayed on.

For several of the stayers, this was a bad decision. After the U.S. interventions of 1982 and 1983, Americans began disappearing off the streets of Beirut, killed or kidnapped. The offensive against American nationals started in early 1984 with the murder of Malcolm Kerr, the president of the American University of Beirut. Kidnappers grabbed three Americans during 1984, including William Buckley, the C.I.A.'s station chief in Lebanon. Buckley was subsequently tortured and killed. Four more Americans were seized in 1985. This group included the director of the American University hospital and the supervisor of Catholic Relief Services in Beirut. During the same period, terrorists bombed the American embassy in Kuwait.

The assassins, kidnappers, and bombers were shadowy figures, but the most important of them evidently belonged to Hezbollah, a radical faction of Shiite Muslims. This group received support from the Iranian government, although the precise nature of the support was impossible to ascertain. Over time a certain tendency toward freelancing among the kidnappers may have developed, but few observers doubted that the Iranian government set the general tone that guided their activities.

For this reason, when the Reagan administration weighed means for gaining the release of the hostages, its thoughts turned to Teheran. The avowed position of the administration toward the kidnappers was complete noncompromise. "The United States gives terrorists no rewards," Reagan declared in June 1985. "We make no concessions. We make no deals." But the truth was otherwise. For several months prior to this statement, officials of the Reagan administration had been designing deals for gaining the hostages' release. The chief deal-makers were members of the staff of the National Security Council, including the president's national security adviser, Robert McFarlane. Their thinking was that the moment had arrived for improved relations between the United States and Iran. Whether Americans liked Khomeini or not, Iran remained the most important and powerful country in the crucial Persian Gulf region. The United States and its allies required access to Persian Gulf oil, and access to Persian Gulf oil required a modicum of stability in the neighborhood of the oil fields. Teheran could help provide that stability. For their part, comparatively moderate elements in the Iranian government presumably would be interested in better relations with Washington, if only because the United States was the source of the military spare parts Iran needed to fight its war against Iraq. As a bonus of improved relations between the United States and Iran, Teheran might arrange the release of the American hostages.[14]

Such was the theory behind what became the Iran-contra affair. Some important groups in the Reagan administration doubted that the theory could be translated into practice. Officials at the State Department, questioning the influence of the hypothesized moderates, thought Teheran wasn't ready for improved relations. The United States made a better foil than friend to the Iranian regime, according to the professional diplomats' view. The Defense Department similarly registered reservations. The Pentagon's analysts disliked the idea of arming any government that continued to denounce the United States and agitate for the overthrow of conservative and moderate governments throughout the Middle East. The C.I.A. conceded that improved relations with Iran might be possible, but, fearing a trap, it wanted to see some solid evidence of Teheran's good faith. The release of the C.I.A.'s William Buckley, still alive at this time, would be a promising first step.

Despite this opposition, McFarlane and C.I.A. director Casey, who was closer to the president than to his own agency, pushed ahead with plans for a rapprochement with Iran. McFarlane wrote up a directive recommending that the administration attempt to forge ties with moderates in Iran. In order to do so, the administration should encourage American allies to help Iran meet its "import requirements," including "selected military equipment."[15]

McFarlane's proposal provoked outrage at the State and Defense Departments. Secretary of State Shultz objected that facilitat-

---

[14]*New York Times,* July 1, 1985.
[15]*Report of the Congressional Committees Investigating the Iran-Contra Affair* (Washington, 1987), 165.

ing the shipment of weapons to the Iran government contradicted clearly enunciated American policy and was "contrary to our interest both in containing Khomeinism and in ending the excesses of this regime." Secretary of Defense Weinberger ridiculed McFarlane's draft directive as "almost too absurd to comment on." Weinberger added, "It's like asking Qaddafi to Washington for a cozy lunch."[16]

McFarlane dealt with the opposition of Shultz and Weinberger by ignoring it. He proceeded with his initiative and declined to apprise the secretaries of what he was doing. To their discredit, they failed—deliberately or inadvertently—to keep careful watch on McFarlane and the N.S.C. staff.

During July or August 1985 (stories recounted after the fact conflicted regarding the precise date), McFarlane pitched his plan to Reagan. The national security adviser timed his effort adroitly, in that his presentation followed shortly a meeting by the president with families of the American hostages in Lebanon. A standard feature of Reagan stump oratory had long been the personal anecdote: the tale of an individual or family touched by tragedy or ennobled by heroism. Reagan succeeded in employing these anecdotes to good effect because he sincerely shared the feelings of the persons whose lives and experiences he described. When it came to the hostages in Lebanon, the president was a pushover for the pleas of the hostages' families to do something to get their loved ones home safe and soon.

McFarlane exploited Reagan's feelings by casting his proposal regarding Iran as a move that might lead to the hostages' release. McFarlane didn't describe the American weapons as ransom for the hostages, but simply suggested that an improvement of relations between Washington and Teheran might open many doors, including those that stood between the hostages and freedom. Reagan approved McFarlane's proposal. (So said McFarlane, and so indicated the balance of evidence gathered later by congressional investigators. Reagan said he couldn't recollect giving his approval.)

McFarlane had already been in contact with Israeli officials, who would act as the administration's agents with Iran. The Israelis met with representatives of the Iranian government and received a request for American TOW antitank missiles. Iraqi armor was inflicting heavy losses on the lightly armed—sometimes essentially un-

---

[16]Ibid.; Caspar W. Weinberger, *Fighting for Peace* (New York, 1990), 363–64.

armed—Iranian forces, and Teheran hoped to level the field. Upon receiving the president's authorization, McFarlane relayed the word to Israel to send the Iranians what they wanted. On August 20, a transport plane departed from Israel with ninety-six TOW missiles. Later the same day it touched down in Teheran, unloaded the missiles, and left.

To McFarlane's chagrin and Reagan's disappointment, the transaction didn't result in the freeing of any of the hostages. The middleman in the exchange, an Iranian expatriate named Manucher Ghorbanifar, explained to McFarlane that there had been a mixup. The wrong group of people in Teheran had gotten the missiles. The commander of the militant Iranian Revolutionary Guards had caught wind of the weapons delivery and stationed troops at the airport. When the missiles arrived, the troops had snatched them before the moderates the missiles were intended for reached the scene. Ghorbanifar told McFarlane not to give up; the next load of weapons would produce a better result.

McFarlane was dubious about Ghorbanifar, who had a checkered background and not much in the way of references. Moreover, Ghorbanifar wasn't working for free: he was charging a commission for his services. Naturally he wanted the business to continue. Oliver North, the N.S.C. staffer who did much of the bag work in the Iran-contra affair, characterized Ghorbanifar in plain language: "I knew, and so did the rest of us who were dealing with him, exactly what Mr. Ghorbanifar was. I knew him to be a liar. I knew him to be a cheat, and I knew him to be a man making enormous sums of money." North then went on to explain why the administration stuck with Ghorbanifar: "We knew what the man was, but it was difficult to get other people involved in these activities."[17]

So McFarlane suppressed his doubts and apparently persuaded Reagan to do likewise. (According, again, to McFarlane. Again, Reagan's later memory failed on the subject.) In mid-September a shipment of more than four hundred TOW missiles left Israel. This time the weapons landed in Tabriz, which, according to Ghorbanifar, was beyond the control of the Revolutionary Guards. And this time the delivery produced at least some of the desired effect. The next day one of the American hostages was freed near the American embassy in Beirut.

[17]Theodore Draper, *A Very Thin Line* (New York, 1991), 264–65.

Although the release of Benjamin Weir was gratifying to his family and friends, the fact that the Iranians had sprung only one hostage in exchange for five hundred missiles must have been discouraging to McFarlane and the other administration officials who knew about the deal. At this point, the effort to buy Teheran's good will might have halted but for the influence of a second factor in the operation: the contra connection.

Since the passage of the 1984 Boland amendment, administration officials had sought various means to circumvent the congressional ban on aid to the Nicaraguan rebels. One method was to dun foreign governments that sought to remain in Washington's good graces. "Tin cup diplomacy," dunner Elliot Abrams later called it. Cooperating governments would provide the assistance Congress had withdrawn. A second method was to solicit donations from wealthy individuals who shared the administration's opinions regarding the worthiness of the contra cause.[18]

A third method was to siphon money from the sale of weapons to Iran and channel it to the contras. Congress didn't know about the weapons sales, and therefore couldn't ask any inconvenient questions about the money.

The contra connection, combined with Reagan's continuing solicitude for the welfare of the hostages and McFarlane's determination to see his initiative turn out successfully, kept the secret arms sales to Iran alive. When the Iranians discovered how much the sales meant to the Americans—although they didn't know the entire reason—they heightened their demands. TOW missiles were well and good, they said, but not sufficient. They needed Hawk anti-aircraft missiles—say, 150 of them. In addition, the Americans should throw in a couple hundred Sidewinder missiles and three or four dozen Phoenix missiles.

McFarlane and his N.S.C. assistants, including Oliver North, thought this was too much. The Iranians would have to show better faith than they had thus far before they would get such a large supply of top-flight American weapons. North proposed a counteroffer. Iran would get eighty Hawks as a down payment. Then, if the Iranians persuaded the hostage-holders to release five Americans and perhaps one French hostage (the release of a non-American would help disguise the scheme), Iran would receive forty more Hawks. To

[18]Ibid., 373.

start the ball rolling, the N.S.C. staffers arranged the delivery of eighteen Hawks from Israel to Teheran. The missiles duly arrived.

The Iranians didn't like North's scheme. They objected that the Americans weren't offering enough missiles and that, anyway, the ones just delivered were the wrong kind. (Evidently the Iranians were confused about the Hawks' capabilities.) They particularly complained about the Israeli markings on the missiles, which had been taken from Israel's stockpile subject to subsequent American replacement. It was bad enough for the Islamic Republic of Iran to have to rely on weapons from the Great Satan, but for those weapons to bear the insignia of the Zionist entity was utterly intolerable. The Iranians sent a message to the Reagan administration via Ghorbanifar: "We have done everything we said we were going to do, and you are now cheating us, and you must act quickly to remedy this situation." Until the Americans did, they could forget about seeing any more hostages freed.[19]

McFarlane and North set about giving Teheran satisfaction. They believed that the administration was in too deep to back out now. The hostages' fate depended on them. North argued, "If we do not make at least one more good try at this point, we stand a good chance of condemning some or all to death." North went on, "While the risks of proceeding are significant, the risks of not trying one last time are even greater." Among these risks was one North didn't mention explicitly, but which must have figured in the thinking of those who knew of the operation: that if they didn't come through with more missiles, Iranian opponents of the arms sales might blow the whistle and reveal the administration's duplicity.[20]

North also failed to mention the money the arms sales to Iran were generating for the contras. Precisely how much money went to the contras via the Iranian channel was never determined by the congressional investigators who later attempted to do so. Estimates ranged up to $16 million. This wasn't a great deal as far as arms aid went, and in fact it was substantially less than North and the other directors of the project had anticipated. But while the project was still under way, North and the others could hope for better. And their hopes drove the project forward despite their disappointments regarding the Iranian end of the business.

[19]*Report of the Congressional Committees Investigating the Iran-Contra Affair*, 187.
[20]Ibid., 194.

By this juncture in the operation, no one who knew of it could doubt that it had become a matter of bartering arms for hostages. North was so blunt as to commit to paper a tally delineating how many weapons were to be exchanged for each batch of hostages:

H-hour: 1 707 w/300 TOWs = 1 AMCIT
H + 10 hrs: 1 707 (same A/C) w/300 TOWs = 1 AMCIT
H + 16 hrs: 1 747 w/50 HAWKS & 400 TOWs = 2 AMCITs
H + 20 hrs: 1 707 w/300 TOWs = 1 AMCIT
H + 24 hrs: 1 747 w/2000 TOWs = 1 French hostage

(Translation: At zero hour, one Boeing 707 jet would deliver three hundred TOW missiles, and one American citizen would be freed. Ten hours later, the same aircraft would deliver three hundred more TOWs, and another American would be released. And so forth.)[21]

Through the first part of 1986, the White House oversaw the sale of one thousand TOW missiles to Iran. To supplement the sales, American intelligence agencies provided critical information, derived from American spy satellites, about the placement and strength of Iraqi armed forces in the Iran-Iraq war.

The Iranians accepted the missiles and intelligence. But, complaining that the weapons were not what they had ordered, they kept the hostages in captivity.

Even so, the operation continued, now driven more than ever by the contra connection. By one after-the-fact estimate, the latest sale of missiles had sent $6 million to the contras, less the substantial commission charged by broker Richard Secord—a commission whose size, like so much else in the Iran-contra affair, was never fully disclosed.

Throughout the spring and summer of 1986, North and John Poindexter, McFarlane's replacement, continued to try to buy the hostages' release. McFarlane, no longer an administration official but still deeply involved in the operation, traveled to Teheran with the first planeload of a new shipment of weapons, this time of spare parts for Hawk missiles. McFarlane hoped to return with the hostages, or at least with guarantees of their imminent release. To celebrate the triumphal conclusion of the long process, he carried a chocolate cake to Teheran. (Anything alcoholic could have offended Iran's Islamic conscience.)

[21]Ibid.

The Iranians quickly quashed McFarlane's hopes. They said they couldn't possibly arrange the release of any hostages until all the Hawk parts had been delivered. McFarlane replied, with equal adamance, that the hostages had to come home first. The meeting ended in a deadlock. McFarlane returned to the United States, with the arms-for-hostages operation apparently at an end.

But the Iranians contrived to keep it going by a timely concession. After McFarlane left, they prevailed upon the hostage-holders to release one more American, Lawrence Jenco. Though McFarlane was thoroughly disenchanted with the Iranians by this point, North and Poindexter took Jenco's release as a sign of Iranian cooperativeness. They ordered the delivery of the balance of the Hawk spare parts.

Through the early autumn of 1986, the arms-for-hostages operation proceeded fitfully. North and Poindexter persisted in hoping for a breakthrough, which never came, although the Iranians kept holding out the possibility that it might. The possibility persuaded the weapons-dealing duo to arrange the shipment of another five hundred TOW missiles to Teheran. A few days later a third American hostage was freed.

Twenty-four hours after this, the arms-for-hostages operation crashed to a stop when a Lebanese newsmagazine spilled the story. The Reagan administration initially denied that it had been selling weapons to Iran in order to secure the release of American hostages. But once American reporters, having been scooped by their Lebanese counterparts, started digging into the affair, administration officials were forced to confess that they had indeed violated their own stated policy of trying to prevent Iran from receiving weapons. They may even have violated American laws restricting trade with Iran. Eventually the contra connection to the arms-for-hostages business came to light, embarrassing all even more.

5. SIDING WITH SADDAM

The cover-blowing of the Reagan administration's arms-for-hostages operation contributed to a tilt in favor of Iraq in the Iran-Iraq war. By the end of 1986, the war in the Persian Gulf had been going on for six horrible years. The Iraqis, who had started the war, albeit upon provocation, had had the better of the fighting during the first two years. After 1982, the balance shifted in favor of Iran, which outstripped Iraq in population, wealth, and devotion to the cause of fundamentalist Islam. The United States had initially adopted a hands-off policy, hoping that neither side would knock out the other and thereby gain a decisive advantage in the Persian Gulf. But as Iran's forces began to inflict heavy defeats on the Iraqis, the Reagan administration worried that Khomeini might actually make good on his threat to replace the secular regime of Saddam Hussein in Baghdad with a militantly Islamic one. Washington responded by upgrading U.S. representation in Iraq and organizing a blockade of weapons to Iran, on the stated reasoning that Iraq accepted the principle of a cease-fire, while Iran didn't. (Simultaneously, of course, administration officials were violating their own avowed policy by selling weapons to Teheran.)

The public American preference for Saddam Hussein grew stronger late in 1986 when Iran intensified attacks on merchant shipping in the Persian Gulf. The purpose of the Iranian attacks was to frighten oil carriers away from Kuwait, the small but oil-saturated Arab emirate at the end of the Gulf, which, while nominally neutral in the war, had been helping finance Arab Iraq against Persian Iran. The Kuwaitis wasted no love on Saddam Hussein, but at the moment they judged Khomeini the greater threat to their safety and wealth.

Kuwait's government reacted to the Iranian attacks by appealing to the great powers for protection. The Soviet Union answered that it would be delighted to assist the Kuwaitis. The Reagan administration had no compelling desire to step into the murderous cross fire between Iran and Iraq, but once the Soviets volunteered for service in the Gulf the administration believed it could do no less. Otherwise the oil states of the region might start looking to Moscow for protection, a development that would represent an intolerable threat to the oil supply of the U.S. alliance system. "I was quite sure that if we did not respond positively to the Kuwaitis," Caspar Weinberger explained after the fact, "the U.S.S.R. would quickly fill the vacuum, and that the Gulf states, already concerned for a number of reasons [such as the fall of the shah] about American reliability, would not be able to deny basing and port facilities to their new protectors."[22]

The Kuwaiti government proposed that Kuwaiti oil tankers be reflagged under American registry and that the U.S. Navy escort the reflagged vessels through the Gulf and the Strait of Hormuz. This

[22]Weinberger, *Fighting for Peace*, 389–90.

would have one of two beneficial results, from Kuwait's standpoint: it would warn the Iranians away from the Kuwaiti ships, or it would bring the Americans into conflict with the Iranians. It might even do both. In any case, the Arab side in the Iraq-Iran conflict would come out ahead.

The Reagan administration accepted the Kuwaiti proposal, with a condition. The Soviet Union had already agreed to a reflagging scheme, and Washington insisted that the Kuwaitis cancel their deal with Moscow. Strategically, the administration wanted to keep the Kremlin from getting even a toe in the Persian Gulf, and tactically America's admirals shuddered to think of U.S. and Soviet warships trying to dodge each other in the Gulf's shallow waters, shooting at Iranian gunboats without hitting each other. The Kuwaitis accepted the American condition, although they did charter a few Soviet ships to carry oil.

The Reagan administration attempted to portray the reflagging and convoying operation as fully in keeping with U.S. neutrality in the war between Iraq and Iran. After all, Kuwait was neutral, and the United States had long stood for the right of neutral nations to carry on their legitimate trade during wartime.

Yet the attempted portrayal fooled no one. Kuwait might be technically neutral, but Kuwait's oil revenues—the real target of the Iranian attacks—bore much of the burden of keeping Iraq in the war. It was indeed true that Washington wished neither side victory in the war, but with Iran poised to win, this wish translated into a current preference for Iraq. The administration's preference became plain in May 1987 when an American ship patrolling the Gulf suffered an unexpected and inexplicable attack from an Iraqi warplane. If the *Stark* had been prepared for the attack, it probably could have defended itself, but as things were, the attack killed thirty-seven American sailors and crippled the ship. Saddam Hussein's government apologized, claiming mistaken identity. The Reagan administration chose to accept the apology, partly because no plausible motive for a deliberate assault presented itself, and partly because Washington didn't want to have to take strong action against Iraq at a time when Iraq was hard-pressed by Iran.

The Iranians complained loudly at the lack of an American response. Teheran asserted, almost certainly correctly, that the Americans would have reacted much more strongly against an Iranian attack, even if accidental. The incident confirmed the conviction of many in Iran that the Americans were unalterably antagonistic to their country.

The *Stark* affair simultaneously convinced many Americans of the inherent dangers of military involvement in the Gulf. Three dozen Americans had been killed—and by forces of the side the United States was supporting. What would happen when the reflagging and convoying operation began in earnest and Americans began exchanging fire with the Iranians? Congressional Democrats and some Republicans talked about invoking the 1973 War Powers Act. Yet largely because no American ground troops were being placed in the cannon's mouth, the legislature declined to press the issue.

It helped the administration that other countries joined the United States in defending the Gulf shipping lanes. Britain and France contributed vessels to the operation, which eased some American minds, if only because the Iranians would have more ships to shoot at should they decide to contest the convoying. The British and French participation also alleviated complaints that U.S. forces were (again) being asked to do for America's allies what the allies should be doing for themselves—in this case, safeguarding oil destined for European and Japanese automobiles, factories, and generating plants.

The convoying operation went fairly smoothly at first but started getting rough during the late summer of 1987. In September an American warship encountered an Iranian minelayer in the act. The American vessel seized the offending craft. A few weeks later an Iranian gunboat fired a rocket at one of the reflagged Kuwaiti tankers, and U.S. ships and planes responded by destroying an Iranian communications post on an offshore oil platform.

Yet the conflict between the United States and Iran didn't quite reach the temperature of combustion. After the deadly and futile intervention in Lebanon, the Reagan administration had no wish to get more deeply involved in the Iran-Iraq war. Protecting the flow of oil down the Gulf was one thing, but escalating to larger violence against Iran was something else. Congress showed no greater enthusiasm for such a venture, and neither did American voters.

Nor did most Iranians apparently care to escalate the fight against the Americans. The Iranian people were exhausted after seven years of war. Some recent battles had gone against Iran's

forces, and common sense, if nothing else, counseled against pro-
voking a new and very powerful foe.

But one person's common sense is another's foolishness, and for
several months radicals in Iran contrived to maintain the pressure
against the Americans. As it had ever since the overthrow of the
shah, the United States served as a bogey for the Islamic hard-liners
in Teheran. Under the leadership of the Iranian Revolutionary
Guards, Iranian forces continued laying mines in the shipping lanes
of the Gulf. One of the mines exploded against a U.S. warship, the
Roberts. The Reagan administration ordered reprisals against Iranian
platforms.

The tanker war produced much tension but comparatively few
casualties until July 1988. In the first week of that month, an American destroyer, the *Vincennes,* detected an Iranian plane approaching
on what seemed to the nervous captain to be a menacing path. The
captain ordered his missile crew to fire on the plane, which exploded
and crashed into the sea. Only afterward did the captain discover
that the plane was a civilian airliner carrying three hundred passen-
gers, all of whom perished.

The U.S. government called the attack a terrible accident, the
sort of thing that happens too often in wartime. Accident it may
have been, but the Iranian government rejected the American explanation and condemned the attack as a monstrous and diabolical
crime.

Even so, Teheran declined to use the attack as a justification for
raising the stakes in the fight against the Americans. At just this
time, the Iranian government was deciding that the war against Iraq
had lasted long enough. Saddam Hussein's secularists in Baghdad
weren't about to fall, and the Islamic revolution would have to
spread by other means. In mid-July 1988 Teheran accepted a United
Nations cease-fire proposal. After eight terrible years the first Gulf
war ended.

The people most relieved by the war's end lived in Iran and
Iraq, but many Americans breathed more easily too. With the fighting's termination, the threat to the tanker traffic in the Gulf essentially disappeared, and with it the threat to the American forces in
the area. Oil began flowing more freely—and therefore more
cheaply. Indeed, odds were that the principals and seconds in the
just-concluded war would pump as much oil as they could, to pay

off the debts incurred during the war. From the perspective of petroleum consumers in Europe, Japan, and North America, that part of the future which hinged on the affairs of the Gulf looked more promising than it had for more than a decade.

6. THE YEN ALSO RISES

From other perspectives, the future looked less promising, at least for Americans. During the 1980s, America's relative economic power continued to slip. The most visible manifestations of the slippage were the country's twin deficits: the federal budget deficit and the national trade deficit. The federal budget deficit—the annual excess of federal spending over federal revenues—had been under development for some time, especially since the latter half of the 1960s, when the war in Vietnam and the War on Poverty in the United States sent federal expenditures to new highs. But the budget deficits of the Reagan era made the deficits of the 1960s and 1970s look like slips of an accountant's pencil. The big military buildup of the first Reagan administration, amplified by the Republicans' passion for trimming tax rates and by increases in social security and other nondefense programs, pushed the federal budget farther out of balance than almost anyone had thought possible just a few years before. During Reagan's first term, Washington went deeper into debt than the federal government had gone during the entire period since the founding of the American republic.

During Reagan's second term, the federal government doubled the debt again. By the end of the 1980s, a historically huge deficit had become part of people's expectations about government and the economy, to the point where fiscal tightwads accepted without complaint deficits that even the loosest liberals wouldn't have dared propose a decade earlier. Politicians, pundits, academics, and others still talked of balancing the federal budget, but they almost never spoke of doing it this year or the next, instead pushing the proposed era of restored virtue into the flexible future. With each year that passed, the future grew more flexible and more distant.

The other deficit, the trade deficit—the excess in value of imports over exports—was less obviously the consequence of decisions made in Washington or, for that matter, any other single place. The trade deficit resulted from the decisions of millions of Americans to purchase foreign products: shoes from Malaysia, dinner plates from China, cars and electronic equipment from Japan, machine tools from Germany, paper from Canada, tomatoes from Mexico, grapes from Chile, steel from Brazil, cobalt from Zaire, diamonds from South Africa, coffee from Guatemala, petroleum from Saudi Arabia. It resulted as well from decisions by millions of foreigners not to buy American products. In certain instances, these latter decisions were made with the assistance of foreign governments, as when Japan restricted agricultural imports from the United States. In certain instances, the foreigners simply preferred non-American products to American, as when Canadian car buyers purchased Hyundais instead of Chevrolets.

Regardless of the influences shaping the decisions, the result was that the gap between what Americans sold to foreigners and what foreigners sold to Americans mounted to more than $100 billion annually during the 1980s. As the foreigners sent their dollars back to the United States in the form of loans and investments, the United States became a net debtor nation for the first time since World War I. In this regard the twin deficits really *were* twins, for U.S. government bonds purchased by foreign banks with deposits from exporters to America helped finance the bulging budget deficit.

Between them, the federal and trade deficits circumscribed the freedom of action of the U.S. government and the United States as a whole. The rising federal deficit squeezed out old government programs that probably would have received funding in flusher times, and prevented the launching of new ones. For example, while most Americans decried the deteriorating condition of American education, Congress declined to provide significant support that might have alleviated the deficiencies. The American space program, which had produced some of the proudest accomplishments of the postwar period, saw its new projects challenged, delayed, reduced, and shelved.

In foreign affairs, the United States no longer possessed the capacity to finance major reconstruction abroad. During the late 1940s, American Marshall Plan dollars had catalyzed the restoration of the West European countries to economic health, and in the process had gone far to curb unwanted political tendencies in those countries. But in the late 1980s, Washington couldn't find the funds to underwrite an analogous program of reconstruction for the Soviet Union. While many economists, historians, and other public thinkers pointed out that $10 billion or so to give perestroika a boost would be a wise investment, especially after the thousands of billions spent over the years to create the conditions in which perestroika became possible, Washington just couldn't find the money. The Soviets might make the transition to democracy and a market economy, or they might not. But Americans would have little influence in the matter.

In the minds of many Americans—and of the sizable group of foreigners who looked to Washington for leadership in dealing with the world's ongoing problems—America's economic difficulties could hardly have developed at a worse time. With the decline of the Soviet Union as a military and political threat, the most usable form of power in world affairs appeared increasingly to be economic. Many people predicted that the new superpowers of the future would be economic dynamos like Japan and Germany.

Japan seemed particularly well placed to pick up where the United States was leaving off. Economically prostrate at the end of World War II, Japan had revived during the late 1940s and 1950s, partly as a result of direct American aid, partly as a result of American military-related spending in Japan during the Korean War, and mostly as a result of the industriousness and cleverness of the Japanese people. During the 1960s Japan emerged as a powerhouse of East Asia, although not yet a major competitor in most world markets. The oil shocks of the 1970s threatened body blows against the Japanese economy, which imported almost all its liquid fuels, but the Japanese turned the tightened energy situation to their advantage by expanding exports of the fuel-efficient cars they had been making for years.

By the beginning of the 1980s Japanese automobiles were stealing a sizable share of the U.S. market. So popular were the Japanese cars with American buyers, and so threatening to American manufacturers, that by the mid-1980s Japan had been persuaded to accept "voluntary" quotas on exports to the United States, lest the American Congress slap mandatory quotas on the Japanese cars. The Reagan administration supported the arrangement, albeit with a show of reluctance and despite the fact that the bargain violated the administration's publicly pronounced free-trade principles. A disillusioned David Stockman, writing after his resignation as Reagan's budget director, complained, "And so the essence of the Reagan Administration's trade policy became clear: Espouse free trade, but find an excuse on every occasion to embrace the opposite."[23]

Japan's export successes in motor vehicles were mirrored in consumer electronics, computer chips, robotics, and other high-tech industries. The Japanese approach to international economics was a distinctive mix of private-sector initiative and state-bureaucratic oversight. Under the guidance of the powerful Ministry of International Trade and Industry (MITI), Japanese investors and corporations pooled resources and expertise to perfect the techniques of manufacture that made Japanese products world leaders in quality. Whereas in the 1950s "Made in Japan" had often been considered synonymous with slipshod production, by the 1980s the phrase was an assurance of top-notch workmanship.

The astonishing growth of Japanese exports had been a major source of the strain that broke the back of the Bretton Woods system during the early 1970s, and their continued growth continued to strain the system of international finance during the 1980s. With Japan running large trade surpluses with the United States and much of Europe, the yen gained strength against other currencies. For a time, Tokyo resisted upward revaluation of the yen, chiefly on the ground that it would make Japan's exports more expensive. Japan's customers, including the United States, had some reasons of their own for not wishing the yen to rise. American leaders generally considered a strong dollar to be a symbol of a strong country, and a strong dollar attracted foreign investment that helped keep American interest rates lower than they would have been otherwise. (On account of the large U.S. federal deficit, American interest rates were high compared to rates in other countries, a fact that contributed to the strength of the dollar.)

But as the Japanese trade surplus continued to widen, the United States and the other industrial nations decided to encourage shifts in international exchange rates. In September 1985, the finance ministers of the United States, Japan, West Germany, Britain, and France agreed to push the dollar down, especially against the yen. This decision triggered a sharp slide of the dollar that continued, somewhat abated, through the end of the 1980s and well into the 1990s. Where one dollar had purchased nearly four hundred yen in 1985, by the summer of 1994 a dollar couldn't buy even one hundred yen.

[23]David A. Stockman, *The Triumph of Politics* (New York, 1986), 172.

The rising yen slowed the expansion of Japan's trade surplus with the United States but didn't reverse it. At first, many Japanese exporters held the line on dollar-denominated prices, simply accepting lower profit margins and aiming to maintain market share. But as American consumers continued to display their appreciation of Japanese quality, many companies' profits climbed back toward their previous levels. If American manufacturers or American government officials had hoped the rising yen would wean American consumers away from Japanese imports, they were badly mistaken. Just as it had survived the oil shocks of the 1970s and emerged stronger than ever, so Japan survived the currency realignments of the 1980s looking more than ever like an economic superpower.

7. REVOLUTION IN EUROPE

The reemergence of Japan constituted a slow-motion revolution. Though it overturned previous economic relationships across the Pacific and around the world, it was many years in occurring. By comparison, the final collapse of the postwar political order in Europe happened all at once. During the last two years of the 1980s, the changes Gorbachev had unleashed in the Soviet Union spilled beyond Soviet borders into the countries of Moscow's East European empire. Having decided to relax the grip of the Soviet government on life within the Soviet Union, Gorbachev found it logical to loosen the grip of the Soviet government on life outside the Soviet Union as well.

Logic aside, Gorbachev had two objectives in exporting glasnost and perestroika. The first was economic. Garrisoning the East European countries cost a lot of money, and Gorbachev expected retrenchment to produce sizable savings. The second reason was political. Gorbachev wanted the East Europeans to experiment with retooling their societies and governments. The Soviet Union could emulate their successes and avoid their mistakes.

The governments of the East European countries weren't especially pleased at what one of Gorbachev's spokesmen called the "Sinatra doctrine" (after the song in which Frank boasted, "I did it my way"). Almost without exception, the East European regimes were extremely unpopular, maintained in power by the overt or implicit backing of the Soviet Red Army. When Gorbachev made it clear that those regimes had lost that backing—declaring that the Soviet Union had "no right, moral or political," to interfere in Eastern Europe—they began scrambling for new sources of legitimacy. The Polish government of General Jaruzelski agreed to let the banned Solidarity movement compete with the Communist party in elections held during June 1989. The elections gave the Solidarity candidates a foothold in the government, which they then used to boot out the Communists. In Hungary, opposition leaders forced the government to grant their organizations legal status, which they likewise used to push the Communists aside. In Czechoslovakia, reformers retired the Communist bosses in favor of a government headed by dissident playwright Vaclav Havel. In Romania, Nicolae Ceausescu wasn't allowed to retire; when the hated dictator tried to flee the country after his troops refused to follow orders to fire on demonstrators, he was captured and summarily executed.[24]

The most symbolically momentous of the revolutionary events of the period transpired in Germany. Upon learning that it was now on its own, the East German Communist leadership dumped the unpopular Erich Honecker for the unknown Egon Krenz. But once the East German people got to know Krenz, he became almost as unpopular as Honecker. Hundreds of thousands of protesters took to the streets to demand greater freedom, including a lifting of restrictions on travel to West Germany. Krenz, hoping to salvage his position, took the dramatic step in November 1989 of throwing open the gates in the Berlin Wall. Within hours, Berliners from both sides were dancing atop that hated symbol of the postwar division of Germany. In the giddiness of the moment, all things seemed suddenly possible—including the reunification of Germany. For two generations, reunification had been a fading prospect, of late hardly mentioned. Now it became possible, then likely, then inevitable. Less than twelve months after the Wall came down, reunification was an accomplished fact.

The revolutions in Eastern Europe in 1989 marked the end of the postwar order in Europe. For more than forty years, the Soviet Union had dominated the destiny of the eastern half of the continent, sometimes by naked force, more often by suggestion of same. No longer. And in renouncing Moscow's right to intervene in East

[24]Michael R. Beschloss and Strobe Talbott, *At the Highest Levels* (Boston, 1993), 134.

European affairs, Gorbachev implicitly loosened America's hold on Western Europe as well. While the Soviet Union had remained a credible threat to West European security, the Atlantic allies had been content—if not always happy—to look to the United States for protection. With the Soviet threat growing less credible by the month, America's European allies felt increasingly free to go their own way. One clear indication of the new freedom in both halves of Europe was the reunification of Germany. For four decades, the superpowers had made certain that no vital decisions were made in either Bonn or East Berlin without the respective concurrence of Washington and Moscow. But in arranging reunification, the two Germanys plunged ahead on their own, leaving the Americans and Soviets to accept a fait accompli.

The end of the postwar order in Europe also signaled the end of the Cold War. American leaders and many of the American people congratulated themselves on their country's triumph over the Soviet Union. They had reason for self-congratulation. For most of two generations, the United States and the Soviet Union had been locked in a struggle for global predominance. The struggle had been ideological and geopolitical, and in both areas the Soviets had been crushed. To be sure, the narrowly military outcome of the geopolitical contest was a draw, with neither side willing to risk nuclear destruction to defeat the other. But the economic outcome of the geopolitical contest was a clear victory for the United States: the Soviet economy had stagnated while the American economy had grown into the largest and most powerful in world history. Ideologically, the Soviet eclipse was even sharper. Communism had been shown to be as bankrupt as the Soviet economy—not least because of that economy's bankruptcy. Communism's apologists had promised to provide a better material life than the capitalists could; with this promise they had attempted to justify their repression of individual liberties. They had failed to deliver, and repudiation was their reward.

Yet if the end of the Cold War eased American worries about the Soviet Union, plenty of worries remained. The Middle East was as turbulent as ever. Indeed, that region was even more turbulent than before, now that the Persian Gulf troubles had been added to the Arab-Israeli conflict. While the U.S. budget deficit limited Washington's flexibility in foreign affairs, America's chronic trade deficit continued to erode America's economic power vis-à-vis its allies. Many observers predicted that with the loss of economic power would come a loss of political power; without question Japan and Germany would feel less beholden to the United States now that the Soviet Union was no longer a serious military threat. Enemies have their virtues, including keeping friends in line.

CHAPTER 5

The Pendulum Breaks: 1989–1995

A question that came to many minds on the morning after the Cold War was what use the United States would make of its status as the sole surviving superpower. Would Washington police the planet, now fearless of Soviet retaliation? Or would Americans retire from the fray, tending to their own narrow security and leaving the rest of the world to fend for itself?

A partial answer emerged before the rubble of the Berlin Wall had been swept away. In the summer of 1990, Saddam Hussein culminated a campaign of psychological warfare against Kuwait by ordering Iraqi troops to invade and occupy the neighboring ministate. The Bush administration responded with alacrity, first sending American forces to the Persian Gulf to prevent additional Iraqi expansion, and then leading an international coalition that rooted the Iraqis out of Kuwait and restored the pre-invasion status quo in the Gulf.

Yet this answer was only partial, for doubts existed regarding the extent to which the Gulf precedent would apply to other conflicts and instances of international ugliness. The doubts grew when the breakup of Yugoslavia triggered a complex of brutal wars and Washington, despite the calls of many in the United States and elsewhere for sending help to the beleaguered Bosnian Muslims, declined to get involved in any substantial way.

Other items of international relations provoked additional disputes regarding America's role in the world. Free-traders tilted against protectionists over the U.S. trade deficit, over relations with Japan and with the increasingly coherent European Community, and over a proposed U.S.-Canadian-Mexican trade pact. Human rights advocates supported sanctions against China for suppressing the civil liberties (and sometimes the lives) of dissidents, while proponents of realpolitik held that to ostracize China would damage American interests and probably backfire against the dissidents as well. Budget-cutters demanded defense downsizing now that the Soviet threat had essentially vanished, but dry-powder types contended that in the fragmented and unpredictable post–Cold War world, the United States needed to remain ready for all manner of military contingencies. As the Soviet Union broke up into its constituent republics, which then attempted to continue the transition to democracy, advocates of economic assistance to the former Soviet peoples argued for American aid to ease the transition, while opponents insisted that the United States needed to invest its resources at home, to rebuild the economy that had made the U.S. victory in the Cold War possible.

1. SADDAM HUSSEIN CHALLENGES THE WORLD

The Persian Gulf crisis of 1990–91 was a delayed consequence of the Gulf war of 1980–88. The outcome of that earlier conflict had been a severe disappointment to Saddam Hussein. The Iraqi regime had failed to establish its hegemony in the Gulf, and had spent a great deal of money in the failure. To pay off some of its debts, Baghdad hoped to persuade its fellow OPEC members to hike the price of petroleum. But countries like Saudi Arabia and Kuwait, possessing far larger oil reserves than Iraq, had a greater stake in the long-term stability of international oil markets. They had seen how the big price increases of the 1970s had driven consumers away from petroleum, toward conservation and alternative energy sources, and they didn't want to risk doing that again. Hussein railed at the price moderates, charging them with conspiring to starve Iraq of the revenues it needed to pay for the late war—which, he declared, it had fought on behalf of all Arabs.

Hussein singled out Kuwait for special criticism. Kuwait was small and relatively defenseless; moreover, Iraq had some long-standing grievances against Kuwait. The Iraqis contended that Kuwait was legitimately part of Iraq and had been stolen away by a cabal of British imperialists and Kuwaiti usurpers. Baghdad resented Kuwaiti control of two islands that hindered Iraqi access to the Gulf, and it accused the Kuwaitis of taking more than their fair share of oil from a field that straddled the frontier between the two countries. The Iraqis had threatened Kuwait with the use of force on a number of previous occasions, but each time had refrained from making the threat good. In July 1990, Hussein threatened Kuwait again, sending some one hundred thousand battle-tested troops to the border region.

In Washington, the administration of George Bush didn't know what to make of Hussein's bullying. Because Iraq had stood down each time before, there was a tendency in Washington to believe that Hussein was bluffing again. Hussein had a reputation for bombast, and for bombast nothing beats mobilizing the military. The American ambassador in Baghdad, April Glaspie, met with Hussein on July 25. What she told the Iraqi leader occasioned disagreement afterward. Glaspie later said she warned Hussein not to resort to military force to settle Iraq's quarrel with Kuwait. As Hussein described the same conversation, the ambassador indicated that the United States didn't desire to get involved in a dispute between Arabs. Regardless of what transpired at the July 25 meeting, the Bush administration unquestionably failed to issue a straightforward public warning to Hussein to leave Kuwait alone.

Washington soon wished it had. On August 2, Iraqi troops poured into Kuwait. Conquering the country required only hours, as Iraqi units swiftly seized Kuwait City and Kuwait's oil fields. The Kuwaiti ruler, Emir Jabir Al-Sabah, managed to escape just ahead of the invaders.

The Iraqi takeover of Kuwait opened the eyes of the Bush administration, much as the Soviet invasion of Afghanistan in 1979 had opened the eyes of the Carter administration. At once, the initiative within the administration shifted from those who urged a low American profile in the Gulf to those who advocated strong action. The C.I.A., embarrassed at having failed to predict Hussein's move into Kuwait, evidently now chose to err on the side of predicting too much. Newspaper reports indicated that C.I.A. director William Webster told Bush that Hussein aimed to invade Saudi Arabia next. If Hussein added Saudi Arabia's oil to Iraq's own and now Kuwait's, he would instantly become one of the most powerful men on earth. Considering Hussein's record for making mischief, this was a grim thought.

During most of the period since 1945, whenever U.S. leaders had fretted about the free flow of oil from the Middle East, their fretting had focused on the Soviet Union. The Soviet Union was now in

THE MIDDLE EAST AND THE WAR AGAINST IRAQ, 1991

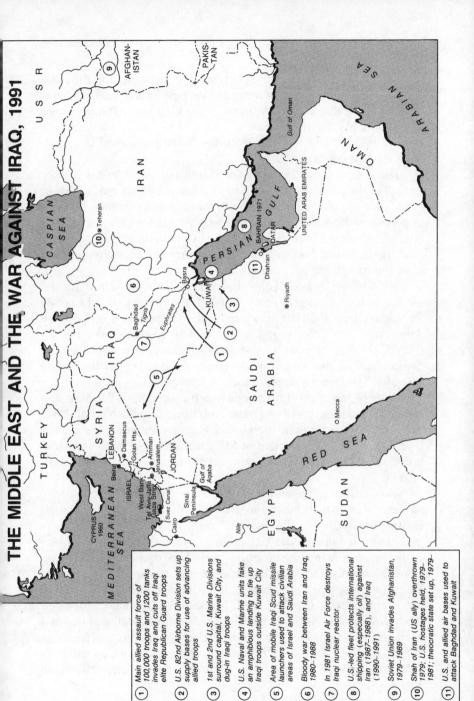

1. Main allied assault force of 100,000 troops and 1200 tanks invades Iraq and cuts off Iraqi elite Republican Guard troops

2. U.S. 82nd Airborne Division sets up supply bases for use of advancing allied troops

3. 1st and 2nd U.S. Marine Divisions surround capital, Kuwait City, and dug-in Iraqi troops

4. U.S. Naval and Marine units fake an amphibious landing to tie up Iraqi troops outside Kuwait City

5. Area of mobile Iraqi Scud missile launchers used to attack civilian areas of Israel and Saudi Arabia

6. Bloody war between Iran and Iraq, 1980–1988

7. In 1981 Israel Air Force destroys Iraqi nuclear reactor

8. U.S.-led fleet protects international shipping (especially oil) against Iran (1987–1988), and Iraq (1990–1991)

9. Soviet Union invades Afghanistan, 1979–1989

10. Shah of Iran (US ally) overthrown 1979; U.S. hostages held, 1979–1981; theocratic state set up, 1979–

11. U.S. and allied air bases used to attack Baghdad and Kuwait

terminal decline, but the principle remained the same, and the Bush administration immediately moved to keep Saddam Hussein's hand off the valves that controlled most of the Gulf's oil. The president dispatched his defense secretary, Dick Cheney, to Saudi Arabia to convince King Fahd that prudence lay in letting several U.S. divisions into his country.

The king did indeed have to be convinced. After Vietnam, after the fall of the shah of Iran, and after the terrorist-induced American evacuation of Lebanon, Fahd didn't place much confidence in Washington's steadfastness. "The Saudis worry whether we're really serious," summarized Brent Scowcroft, Bush's national security adviser. And the last thing Fahd wanted was to provoke Hussein and then have the Americans get nervous and leave.[1]

But Cheney assured Fahd that if Hussein wanted a fight, the United States would give him one. Fahd reportedly pressed Cheney for a guarantee that Hussein wouldn't survive a war against the Americans. Precisely what Cheney said in response was not reported, although it must have satisfied the king, who approved the deployment of the Americans in Saudi Arabia. Within hours, the first of 125,000 troops were on their way.

What began as an effort to deter an Iraqi attack on Saudi Arabia soon evolved into something more ambitious. The Bush administration lobbied hard within the United Nations for sanctions against Iraq. The British government of Margaret Thatcher endorsed sanctions enthusiastically, while France lent somewhat less fervent support.

Most crucial to the anti-Iraq united front was the backing of the Soviet Union, which heretofore had usually lined up opposite the United States in Middle Eastern conflicts. But Gorbachev now placed much hope in the U.S. alliance system's good will, potentially convertible into the economic assistance necessary for the leap from communism to capitalism and democracy, and he abandoned longtime protégé Iraq in favor of the American-led coalition. With the Kremlin's concurrence, the U.N. Security Council condemned the invasion of Kuwait, demanded Iraq's withdrawal, and ordered economic sanctions designed to compel Baghdad to comply.

Having enlisted the Soviet Union and the Security Council on its side, and with U.S. troops on the ground in Saudi Arabia, the Bush

---

[1]Bob Woodward, *The Commanders* (New York, 1991), 251.

George Bush explains his plans for defending
Saudi Arabia to Saudi foreign minister, Prince
Saud al-Faisal. James Baker backstops Bush.
Bush Presidential Materials Project.

administration moved toward forcibly evicting Iraq from Kuwait.
The president ordered American troop strength in Saudi Arabia increased to half a million, with corresponding increases in air and
naval strength. Bush hoped not to have to use all the troops, planes,
and ships; he hoped to frighten Hussein into pulling out of Kuwait
without a fight. But if the Iraqi leader held tough, Bush wanted to be
ready to slam him.

Congress hesitated to follow the president's lead. Few senators
or representatives were eager to send American soldiers into battle

in a region that had just experienced the bloodiest war of the second half of the twentieth century. And even after two decades, the specter of Vietnam hung over Capitol Hill. Senator William Cohen of Maine, a Republican, repeated Mark Twain's observation that while a man would fight to defend his home, he'd feel differently about a boardinghouse. "Right now," Cohen said, "the American people are not persuaded that Kuwait is in fact our home, or Saudi Arabia's our home, but rather the equivalent of the boardinghouse." The U.N.-ordered economic sanctions hadn't really had time to work yet. "Why are we willing to die for the Kuwaitis at this moment?"[2]

But Bush was adamant, and he pressed still harder for military action. The president and his advisers worried that the coalition arrayed against Iraq wouldn't hold together long enough for the sanctions to bite. Conservatives in the Soviet Union, who already were objecting to playing second fiddle to the Americans on the Gulf issue, might force Gorbachev to change his stand. Indeed, at the height of the prewar tension, Soviet foreign minister Eduard Shevardnadze, a strong advocate of the anti-Iraq measures in the U.N., came under such intense political attack that he felt obliged to resign. In several Third World countries where governments supported the United States against Iraq, the people often sympathized with Saddam Hussein, who was portraying himself as the opponent of the imperialistic great powers and the champion of the smaller nations. The Bush administration wasn't sure how long the governments in question could defy the popular sympathies.

In the end, the administration carried the day against the skeptics. By a close vote—in the Senate the margin was five—Congress approved a resolution authorizing the president to use military force to effect the liberation of Kuwait.

A January 15 deadline set by the Security Council came and went, and Iraq's troops stayed in Kuwait; just hours later Bush ordered U.S. forces to attack. Tomahawk cruise missiles delivered the first blows, against targets in and around Baghdad. American warplanes followed, aided by electronic-warfare devices that jammed, blinded, and overloaded Iraqi air defenses and guided American bombs and missiles to their targets with unprecedented accuracy. New "stealth" technology made American F-117As virtually invisi-

[2]Ibid., 339.

ble to Iraqi radar. In the early hours of the war, some Iraqi planes scrambled to challenge the attackers, but Hussein's air force was woefully overmatched in numbers and firepower, and many of those Iraqi planes that weren't blasted at once ended up in Iran, to which their pilots flew for safety. (The fact that the Iraqi pilots chose Iran, the country they had fought against for eight years, was one irony among many surrounding the Gulf War of 1991.)

American planes did most of the fighting during the air phase of the war, but aircraft from Britain, France, Saudi Arabia, and Kuwait also joined the battle. For five weeks coalition aircraft flew thousands upon thousands of sorties against targets in Iraq and Kuwait. Although the Pentagon apparently (and probably partly inadvertently) exaggerated the success of the air offensive, the bombing drastically diminished Iraq's ability to remain in Kuwait, and fairly well shattered its will to do so.

The Iraqis briefly threw a fright into Washington by launching Scud ballistic missiles against Saudi Arabia and Israel. In neither country did the missiles do much damage, but those launched against Israel raised fears of Israeli retaliation, which might have allowed Saddam Hussein to recast the conflict as part of the ongoing Arab struggle against the Zionists. Under extreme American pressure, the Israelis ignored the provocation and refused to retaliate. The Bush administration encouraged Israeli forbearance by rapid delivery of Patriot antimissile missiles, which didn't actually do much to stop the incoming Scuds but did let the Israeli government claim that it was taking action to defend the Israeli people.

After five weeks of the air war, Bush unleashed American ground forces. American tanks and personnel carriers, accompanied by units from other coalition states, swept into Kuwait and Iraq and smashed Hussein's best fighters. American transport helicopters leapfrogged over the Iraqi lines, landing troops forty miles to the rear, where they severed Iraqi supply lines and wreaked general havoc. Iraqi soldiers surrendered by the thousands, while scores of thousands—perhaps one hundred thousand—were killed. Coalition casualties were extremely light for such a major engagement, numbering in the low hundreds.

On February 27, coalition forces liberated Kuwait City. Hours later, Bush called off the attack. This decision occasioned considerable controversy, in that it left Hussein in power. But the coalition had accomplished the objective established by the Security Council,

The war room: George Bush is in the multinational jogging jacket at the
left side of the table, flanked by Dick Cheney and Vice President Dan
Quayle; Colin Powell and Gulf War commander Norman Schwarzkopf
wear the generals' stars across the table; James Baker is to Powell's right;
National Security Adviser Brent Scowcroft is to his left.
Bush Presidential Materials Project.

and the president was willing to settle for the victory already won.
He didn't desire to see American troops fighting street-to-street
through Baghdad, and he hoped that disillusioned Iraqis would topple Hussein and save Washington the trouble.

2. *THE LAST DAYS OF THE SOVIET UNION*

Saddam Hussein must have been relieved that Bush didn't order
U.S. forces to march to Baghdad, but in other respects he might have
considered himself unlucky, or at least the victim of bad timing. Had
this most recent crisis in the Persian Gulf come to a head only a little earlier or later, the alignment of the United States and the Soviet
Union against Iraq might never have occurred. During the Cold
War, Moscow had reflexively obstructed the efforts of the United
States; it almost certainly would have vetoed a Security Council resolution calling for war against Iraq. Had the crisis in the Gulf happened just months later, there would have been no Soviet Union for
the United States to align with. (The government of Russia, the in-

heritor of the Soviet Union's Security Council veto, might have backed the United States, but only with greater political difficulty.)

The breakup of the Soviet Union resulted from the same forces that had caused the breakup of Moscow's East European empire. When inhabitants of the various republics that composed the Soviet Union saw the East Germans, Poles, Hungarians, and the rest going their merry way, they decided that they ought to be able to do the same. The Baltic republics of Lithuania, Latvia, and Estonia were the first to insist on independence. Of all the republics that constituted the union, the Baltics possessed the most persuasive claim to independence, having been incorporated into the Kremlin's realm only in 1940. During the summer of 1989, the Lithuanian parliament declared the 1940 annexation of Lithuania by the Soviet Union illegal. Latvia and Estonia followed shortly.

Without putting public pressure on Gorbachev, the Bush administration encouraged the Soviet government to grant the Balts their freedom. "Cut the Baltics loose," Secretary of State James Baker advised Shevardnadze. "You'd be better off with three little Finlands." (Baker was referring to the fact that Finland, as the price of its independence under Moscow's shadow, had long trod carefully with respect to Soviet sensitivities.)[3]

Gorbachev declined Baker's advice. On the contrary, after a declaration of independence by the Lithuanian parliament in March 1990, he denounced the declaration as illegitimate and invalid. When Latvia followed Lithuania's lead and likewise declared independence, Gorbachev directed a similar denunciation at the Latvians. At the beginning of 1991, just as the crisis in the Persian Gulf was coming to a boil—a coincidence that caught the attention of many veteran Kremlin-watchers—Moscow ordered Soviet units to seize various buildings in Vilnius, the Lithuanian capital. An armed clash between Lithuanian separatists and Soviet units resulted in at least fifteen Lithuanian deaths. A few days later, another confrontation, in the Latvian capital, Riga, left four Latvians dead. Gorbachev tried to dodge responsibility for the violence but succeeded chiefly in raising doubts regarding his control of the Soviet military.

Those doubts grew stronger during the first half of 1991 and crescendoed in August, when a group of disgruntled officers and apparatchiks attempted to overthrow Gorbachev and reverse his re-

[3]Michael R. Beschloss and Strobe Talbott, *At the Highest Levels* (Boston, 1993), 110–11.

forms. For months rumors of an anti-Gorbachev coup had set Moscow abuzz. Some of the rumors were doubtless disinformation planted by Soviet conservatives to scare Gorbachev away from his more ambitious measures. Though Gorbachev did back off a little, he didn't satisfy the hard-line opposition. On August 18, shortly before the scheduled signing of a new treaty redefining the relationship between the central government and the republics, several of the hard-liners took advantage of Gorbachev's temporary absence from Moscow to strike for power. Calling themselves the State Committee for the State of Emergency, they placed him under arrest at his vacation house on the Black Sea and announced that they were taking control of the government.

The Bush administration responded cautiously to the coup. Like Reagan, Bush had developed a liking for Gorbachev and believed that America would benefit from his remaining in power. Bush listened intently as some of his advisers advocated efforts to restore Gorbachev to office. Robert Strauss, the newly appointed ambassador to the Soviet Union, thought out loud regarding what he might do on arrival in Moscow: "I guess I *could* tell those motherfucking sons of bitches off!" But Bush didn't want to go that far. He judged that the United States needed to be prepared to deal with whoever wound up controlling the affairs of the Soviet Union; he didn't want to alienate the new people. He spoke carefully to reporters in describing the ongoing events in the Soviet Union as "extraconstitutional" rather than unconstitutional. Pointing out that the new group in Moscow had publicly affirmed its commitment to continued reform, the president remarked, "I don't know whether to take heart or not. I think what we do is simply watch the situation unfold, and we state and restate our principles, and we'll see where matters go. It's all still unfolding."[4]

So it was, and as it unfolded, the coup fell apart. Boris Yeltsin, the president of the Russian republic, rebuked the instigators of the coup. Yeltsin took courage from the crowd of tens of thousands who rallied to the cause of constitutional government, and who shouted "Shame! Shame!" at the drivers of the tanks the coup makers had sent to surround the parliament building in Moscow. Rows of middle-aged women brandished placards exhorting, "Soviet soldiers: Don't shoot your mothers!" Yeltsin called for a general strike in de-

[4]Ibid., 427–29.

fiance of the coup. Though no friend of Gorbachev—quite the contrary—he demanded Gorbachev's restoration.[5]

The leaders of the coup evidently hadn't anticipated such vigorous opposition, and within a day they lost their nerve. Yeltsin's supporters arrested several of those involved, and Gorbachev flew back to Moscow. Three days after it started, the coup was merely a bad memory. One of the instigators was heard to mutter, upon being led to jail, "Everything is clear now. I am such an old idiot. I've really fucked up."[6]

Though Gorbachev regained his position as president of the Soviet Union, the real hero of the hour was Yeltsin. And though Gorbachev once more headed the government of the Soviet Union, that government was growing increasingly hollow. The almost farcical nature of the coup revealed the enervation of the central government and emboldened separatists in the republics to press for independence. The central government offered little meaningful resistance.

Washington played a distinctly minor role in the final act of the history of the Soviet Union. In September 1991, the Bush administration formally recognized the independence of the Baltic states. This action was motivated less by a desire to promote the disintegration of the Soviet Union than by a hope of guiding the disintegration. As Bush explained, "I don't want to be part of making a mistake that might contribute to some kind of anarchy inside the Soviet Union." Administration officials quietly reminded reporters that there still existed thousands of nuclear weapons on Soviet soil, and anarchy in the midst of such an arsenal was not something to take lightly.[7]

On the other hand, there seemed no percentage in resisting what seemed to be an irresistible movement toward the independence of the republics. Ukraine declared independence just days after the failure of the August coup; several other republics quickly followed suit. Gorbachev and the Soviet parliament scrambled to find a formula that would appease the separatists without utterly eradicating the union; they proposed a loose confederation, with self-government for the republics in most matters but central coordination of

[5]David Remnick, *Lenin's Tomb* (New York, 1993), 481.
[6]Ibid., 490.
[7]Beschloss and Talbott, *At the Highest Levels*, 443.

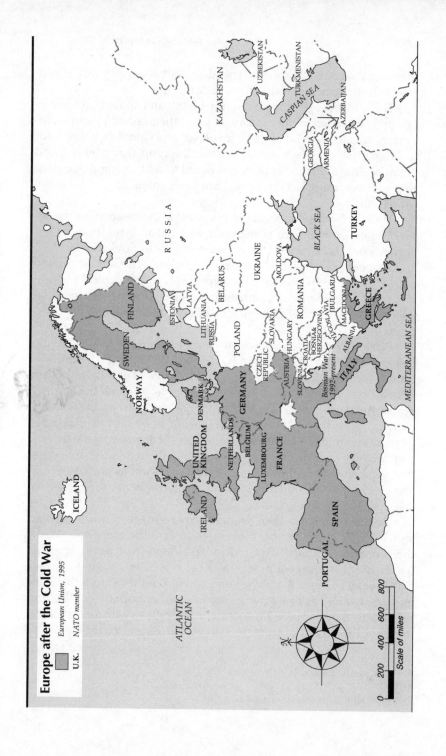

Europe after the Cold War

☐ European Union, 1995
U.K. *NATO member*

ICELAND

ATLANTIC
OCEAN

N
W E
S

Scale of miles
0 200 400 600 800

PORTUGAL SPAIN

IRELAND

UNITED
KINGDOM

NETHERLANDS

BELGIUM

LUXEMBOURG

FRANCE

NORWAY

SWEDEN

FINLAND

DENMARK

GERMANY

CZECH
REPUBLIC

AUSTRIA

SLOVENIA
CROATIA
BOSNIA&
HERZEGOVINA
Bosnian War,
1992-present

ITALY

ALBANIA

GREECE

MACEDONIA

YUGOSLAVIA

BULGARIA

HUNGARY

SLOVAKIA

POLAND

RUSSIA

ESTONIA
LATVIA
LITHUANIA

BELARUS

UKRAINE

MOLDOVA

ROMANIA

BLACK SEA

TURKEY

MEDITERRANEAN SEA

GEORGIA

ARMENIA

AZERBAIJAN

CASPIAN SEA

KAZAKHSTAN

UZBEKISTAN

TURKMENISTAN

R U S S I A

foreign policy and defense. The separatists laughed and rudely told Moscow what it could do with its confederation.

The disintegrative forces became overwhelming as 1991 drew to a close. In early December, Yeltsin consulted with the leaders of Ukraine and Belarus, and together they pronounced the Soviet Union dead. They recommended the establishment of something called the Commonwealth of Independent States, a nebulous association of those republics that cared to join. The leaders of the other republics accepted the idea. Bowing to the inevitable, Gorbachev resigned as president of the Soviet Union. With his resignation, the Soviet government essentially ceased to exist.

3. BALKAN NIGHTMARES

For all the concerns of the Bush administration regarding the potential for anarchy in what became the former Soviet Union, Americans generally applauded the dismantling of their longtime foe. A government that couldn't even hold itself together, most Americans reasoned, couldn't pose much of a threat to other countries. Moreover, the independence of the former Soviet republics appeared to be a triumph for self-determination, a principle Americans had traditionally espoused.

Elsewhere in the eastern half of Europe, the drive for self-determination took a nastier and more brutal turn. The disintegration of Yugoslavia wasn't exactly a consequence of the end of the Cold War; it had been in the works for a decade, at least since the 1980 death of Josip Broz Tito. Tito's local reputation as the great hero of World War II, together with his shrewd balancing of diverse groups and interests, had sufficed to hold together the patchwork of peoples, cultures, and religions that made up Yugoslavia. But following Tito's death, the patchwork began to fray. It did so slowly at first, then gained speed as the various provinces of Yugoslavia reassessed their circumstances amid all the other realignments taking place in Europe in the late 1980s and early 1990s. In 1991 Slovenia and Croatia declared independence. This move infuriated the Yugoslavian federal government and army, which were dominated by Serbia. The Serbs sent troops against Croatia, touching off a series of wars among the components of the erstwhile Yugoslavian federation.

The most bitter and destructive of these wars took place on the soil of Bosnia and Herzegovina, the doubly monikered republic just to Serbia's west. The bitterness and destruction resulted from the desire of ethnic Serbs resident in Bosnia (as it was called for convenience) to attach themselves to neighboring Serbia. The Bosnian Serbs, aided by their cousins in Serbia, waged a scorched-earth offensive against the Bosnian Muslims who had the misfortune of living in the territory the Serbs coveted. Serb tactics included a campaign of "ethnic cleansing," which amounted to an effort to drive out the Muslims by means of murder, rape, and other forms of terrorism. Despite the condemnation of much of the world, the Serb campaign largely succeeded, and Muslim refugees fled the regions controlled by the Serbs. For months that stretched into years, Serb units besieged the Bosnian capital of Sarajevo, inflicting severe damage on the city and tremendous suffering upon its population.

The war in Bosnia prompted yet another reappraisal of American foreign policy. While the crisis in the Persian Gulf had provoked considerable controversy, a consensus came fairly readily that American national interests were jeopardized by Saddam Hussein's actions and evident ambitions. At one point in November 1990 James Baker had declared, "If you want to sum it up in one word: it's jobs." As his listeners understood, what Baker meant was that the American economy couldn't reliably prosper in a world in which a malevolently unpredictable person like Hussein controlled a large portion of the oil supply. Despite Bush's admonitions about creating a "new world order" in which weak countries would be free from fear of predation by the strong, the hard core of American support for action against Hussein rested on this readily identifiable material interest.[8]

Bosnia's misfortune was that it possessed neither oil nor anything else of vital importance to Americans or other influential foreigners. A sizable minority of American officials and opinion shapers contended that Bosnia's lack of commercial commodities shouldn't prevent the United States from going to the Bosnian Muslims' aid. This group took the new-world-order rhetoric seriously. Some likened the Serbs' "ethnic cleansing" to the Nazis' genocide of the Jews and equated the failure of the United States and the other democracies to assist Bosnia to the 1930s failure to halt Hitler. Some

[8]Lawrence Freedman and Efraim Karsh, *The Gulf Conflict 1990–1991: Diplomacy and War in the New World Order* (Princeton, N.J., 1993), 224.

Bosnia advocates called for direct American military intervention, in the form of air strikes or even the introduction of ground troops. Others would have settled for a lifting of the international embargo of arms to the warring parties. The embargo, they claimed, prevented the Bosnian Muslims from defending themselves against the better-equipped Serbs.

Opponents of American involvement in the Bosnian war cited various reasons for their opposition. They pointed to the complexity of the Bosnian terrain in contending that military intervention would be costly and difficult—far more difficult, for instance, than intervention in the open desert of Iraq and Kuwait had been. They noted the obvious determination of the Serbs and asserted that only a political settlement could come close to guaranteeing lasting peace between Serbs and Muslims (and Bosnian Croats), and that military intervention would be futile in the absence of such a political settlement. Indeed, they said, foreign military intervention might even be counterproductive, in that it could cause the war to spread into regions heretofore spared the worst of the conflict. As to the arms embargo, they contended that the only thing its repeal would accomplish would be the prolonging of the fighting, as the Bosnian Muslims got their chance to kill as many as they had lost.

Moreover, while the Gulf crisis had found the United States and the Soviet Union in agreement, the situation in Bosnia promised to be more divisive. For centuries the government of Russia had considered itself the protector of the Slavic and Orthodox Serbs. Exactly what the current Russian government would do if the United States took strong action on the Bosnian question was unclear. But neither the Bush administration nor, after January 1993, that of Bill Clinton could count on Moscow's cooperation. Finally, many people in the United States argued that the problems in the Balkans were Europe's problems. For the four decades of the Cold War, the United States had looked after Europe. It was high time the Europeans started looking after themselves.

Both the Bush administration and, through the start of 1995, the Clinton administration found the arguments of the opponents of military intervention more persuasive than the arguments of its advocates. The resounding lack of popular enthusiasm for intervention doubtless contributed to the opponents' persuasiveness. While both administrations supported various U.N. initiatives to ease the plight of the Bosnians and pressure the Serbs politically to curtail their offensives, neither took the step of committing American combat troops directly to the battle. At one point during the summer of 1993, the Clinton administration made noises about air strikes against Serb positions outside Sarajevo, but the Serbs retreated before the administration needed to decide whether to follow through on its threat. Additional atrocities against the Bosnian Muslims in February 1994 prompted a sharper warning, this by NATO collectively. The shooting down of two Serbian planes by American jets underlined the Clinton administration's seriousness. The Serbs stopped shelling the Bosnian capital and approached the peace table, momentarily reducing the pressure for deeper American intervention. Fighting soon resumed, however, causing Congress, in the autumn of 1994, to force the Clinton administration to stop preventing Bosnia from receiving weapons. This move strained U.S. relations with the rest of NATO; it did little to halt the Balkan war.

4. LESSER CONFLICTS, LESSER VICTORIES

At the heart of the debate over Bosnia was the question of when to use American military force in conflicts overseas. This question, of course, had been at the heart of all the thinking and rethinking about American foreign policy since Vietnam. In the early aftermath of the Gulf War of 1991, the Bush administration congratulated itself that its actions had lifted the shadow of Vietnam from the American collective consciousness. What administration officials meant was that the United States no longer was afraid to use military force in worthwhile causes.

To some extent, the self-congratulation was in order. The administration had indeed overcome the objections of naysayers and orchestrated a brilliant victory over Saddam Hussein—although the brilliance dimmed somewhat during the next four years, as Hussein stubbornly hung on to power in Baghdad and often made nasty gestures in the direction of Washington.

Yet to some degree the self-congratulation missed the point. After Vietnam (as before Vietnam, and always), the issue wasn't whether Americans were afraid to use military force in worthwhile causes, but rather what constituted worthwhile causes. To be sure, Americans after Vietnam set more stringent standards regarding worthwhileness than before, and they calculated costs more carefully against benefits. But very few Americans abjured all use of military force overseas; pacifism has never developed a large constituency in America. When the benefits to the United States appeared likely to outweigh the costs, the American people were willing to countenance military action; thus their support of the Bush administration against Iraq in 1991. When the costs appeared likely to outweigh the benefits, Americans frowned on military intervention; thus their lack of enthusiasm for action in Bosnia in 1992 and after.

The Persian Gulf crisis wasn't the only instance where the benefits of military intervention seemed—at least to the Bush administration—to outweigh the costs. In December 1989 the Republican president ordered an invasion of Panama. Washington had accepted Manuel Noriega's cooperation against the Nicaraguan Sandinistas during the early 1980s but had gradually grown disenchanted with the Panamanian strongman. Noriega had ties to the hemispheric trade in illegal drugs, and though the Reagan administration had been willing to overlook those ties so long as Noriega seemed useful, he had become an embarrassment and a liability at about the time the Iran-contra scandal made almost everything connected to the contra war embarrassing. Noriega responded to his fall from favor with Washington by adopting the mantle of Panamanian patriot confronting the colossus of the north. He didn't convince very many of his compatriots, a majority of whom resented his hijacking of the country's political system. Goon squads, acting in broad daylight in front of the cameras of reporters from around the world, beat up the presidential and vice presidential candidates of the leading opposition party in elections held in May 1989. Noriega's soldiers watched the attacks and did nothing. When the opposition won the elections by a large margin, Noriega annulled the results.

The Bush administration initiated a psychological and diplomatic offensive to drive Noriega from office. The president deployed additional troops to the U.S.-controlled Panama Canal Zone, recalled the American ambassador in Panama City, and publicly urged the Panamanian people to overthrow the dictator. "The problem," Bush said simply, "is Noriega." Tension escalated during the last months of 1989 and reached the snapping point when Noriega's troops shot and killed an unarmed American soldier.[9]

[9]*New York Times*, May 14, 1989.

Bush interpreted the shooting, after the various other outrages committed by Noriega, as sufficient reason for direct military action. On December 19, the president ordered ten thousand U.S. troops into Panama proper. The objective of the invasion, Bush said, was the protection of Americans, the restoration of Panamanian democracy, and the arrest of Noriega, who besides being a blight on Panama had by now been indicted by a U.S. court on drug-trafficking charges. Colin Powell, the chairman of the Joint Chiefs of Staff, was more frank in privately explaining the expected result of the invasion. "We are going to own the country for several weeks," he said.[10]

Taking possession was swift but not clean. Although organized resistance to the American troops was short-lived, the invasion provoked widespread arson and looting in Panama City, and hundreds of Panamanian civilians died. Noriega eluded immediate capture by ducking into the house of the diplomatic representative of the Vatican. American psychological-warfare experts resorted to irregular tactics, including the playing of loud rock 'n' roll music, which Noriega was known to despise, to drive him out of his hiding place. After a ten-day standoff, and following assurances that the charges he faced in the United States did not carry the death penalty, Noriega surrendered. (Following a long trial in Miami, he was convicted and sent to an American prison.)

American troops returned to their bases after handing control over the Panamanian government to the winners of the May elections. Although most Latin American governments denounced the invasion of Panama as high-handed, most Panamanians seemed relieved that Noriega was gone, even if they mourned the many lives lost and the great deal of property damaged in the invasion.

Halfway around the world from the Caribbean, Bush sent U.S. marines into action in rather different circumstances. The countries of the Horn of Africa—principally Ethiopia, Sudan, and Somalia—had been on the verge of famine for most of the 1980s. The importance of the contributing factors varied from year to year and place to place. Sometimes drought was the principal culprit; sometimes bureaucratic inefficiency and corruption; sometimes civil war. In Somalia in 1992, fighting among several rival clans, compounded by bad harvests and weak government, placed a large portion of the

---

[10]Woodward, *The Commanders*, 169.

population at risk of severe malnutrition and even starvation. International aid organizations delivered emergency food to Somalia, only to watch the clans' troops seize the supplies and ration them out at extortionate prices. Those who couldn't pay went hungry. Many died.

Despairing that the Somalian government could bring order to the country and guarantee delivery of the food, the Bush administration decided to send American soldiers to do the job. In December 1992 the U.N. Security Council conferred its blessing on an international operation led by U.S. forces, and shortly thereafter the first American units splashed ashore at Mogadishu. Within weeks, more than twenty-five thousand American soldiers were on Somalian soil.

Few Americans criticized the deployment of American soldiers for such obviously humanitarian ends, and most applauded as the troops swept the streets clear of the gunmen who had been intimidating the Somali populace. The sight of Somali children eating their first square meal in months warmed many hearts in the United States and elsewhere.

But the situation grew more complicated as the Americans found themselves shooting Somalis—mostly bandits and others engaged in antisocial activities, but occasionally innocent bystanders. The clan leaders who at first had ordered their troops to retreat before the American incursion now began putting up greater resistance, inflicting casualties and some deaths on the U.S. contingent. Although the American presence diminished to a few thousand troops in early 1993, as soldiers from other countries joined the U.N. force, the goals of the remaining Americans, as well as of the whole U.N. force, got fuzzier by the week. The foreign soldiers couldn't guarantee the delivery of the relief supplies without taking on the clans, but if they took on the clans they risked deeper involvement in the seemingly bottomless swamp of Somalia's politics. No one responsible was calling Somalia another Vietnam, if only because Somalia's population was much smaller and because of the absence of Cold War overtones to the troubles there. But the sinking feeling that came from discerning no clear end to American involvement in a foreign military intervention was distressingly familiar.

Bill Clinton, much like Lyndon Johnson thirty years before, determined not to get distracted from his agenda of domestic reform by an engagement overseas. Unlike Johnson, Clinton decided to withdraw U.S. forces. In the autumn of 1993 he announced a six-month time limit on the further presence of American soldiers in Somalia. In March 1994 the last of the troops (save for a few dozen embassy guards) came home.

5. LOOKING TOWARD THE TWENTY-FIRST CENTURY

To the thinking of many Americans, the operation in Somalia summarized the difficulties of making foreign policy in the 1990s. Simple humanitarianism motivated the initial American involvement, but American soldiers and American leaders soon discovered that humanitarianism was far from simple. To feed the hungry required fighting the greedy, and often it was difficult to tell the two groups apart. After Americans started killing Somalis and getting killed in return, the old questions about what really constituted vital American interests and how those interests should be defended began being asked again.

The questions arose in a variety of circumstances during the early 1990s. One set involved China. The promising opening of relations with China during the Nixon years had been followed by a phase of stickiness. Nixon's fall, a power struggle in Beijing after Mao Zedong's 1976 death, and the revival of hard-line anticommunism in Washington under Reagan, among other developments, had kept U.S.-Chinese relations tepid—neither warm nor cold. By the second half of the 1980s, however, things seemed to be improving. China was liberalizing economically, moving rapidly toward a market economy; optimists in the West could hope that economic liberalization would lead to political liberalization.

But in the spring of 1989 many optimists were forced to reconsider. For weeks demonstrators had been gathering in Beijing's Tiananmen Square demanding democratic reforms. As a symbol of what they wanted, the demonstrators raised a replica of the American Statue of Liberty. The Chinese government tolerated the protest for a time but in early June it sent tanks and troops to clear Tiananmen Square. A bloodbath ensued in which hundreds of demonstrators were killed.

The Bush administration pondered the appropriate American response. Committed advocates of human rights demanded that

Washington register its outrage at Beijing's bloody-handedness by diplomatic and economic sanctions. Debate centered on China's most-favored-nation status in American international trade, a commercial category that granted China access to American markets on terms as good as those enjoyed by any other country. Supporters of continued most-favored-nation status asserted that the road to reform in China lay in the direction of closer ties to the rest of the world, not in the direction of ostracism. An ostracized China, according to this view, would be an even more intolerant China. Besides, if the United States wouldn't trade with China, other nations would, and American businesses would lose out.

George Bush accepted this reasoning in approving continued most-favored-nation status for China, and so did Bill Clinton. As of early 1995, the Chinese government hadn't conspicuously loosened political restraints, but the Communist old guard in Beijing was getting older all the time. Nominally retired but still dominant Deng Xiaoping was pushing ninety, and Washington looked to the generation that would follow Deng and his octogenarian associates.

It was significant that the primary instrument used to encourage change in China was the economic device of most-favored-nation status. Economic matters had always been important in American foreign affairs, but during the Cold War they were frequently pushed aside in favor of ideological and military considerations and instruments. With the crackup of the Soviet Union, economics increasingly shaped the thinking of American leaders.

Such was definitely the case with respect to American policy toward China's neighbor Japan. As long as the Soviet Union had been a looming presence to Japan's northwest, Tokyo had tended to defer to Washington. Deference hadn't necessarily implied subservience, and tensions on trade and other economic issues had occasionally surfaced in U.S.-Japanese relations. But with the end of the Cold War, those tensions became the most noticeable aspect of dealings between the two countries. Though the dollar continued to fall against the yen, the American trade deficit with Japan continued to grow. American importers charged the Japanese with "dumping" computer chips and other commodities in the United States at prices below the cost of production. American exporters claimed that Japan unfairly hindered sales of American goods in Japan. For their part, the Japanese contended that American products were care-

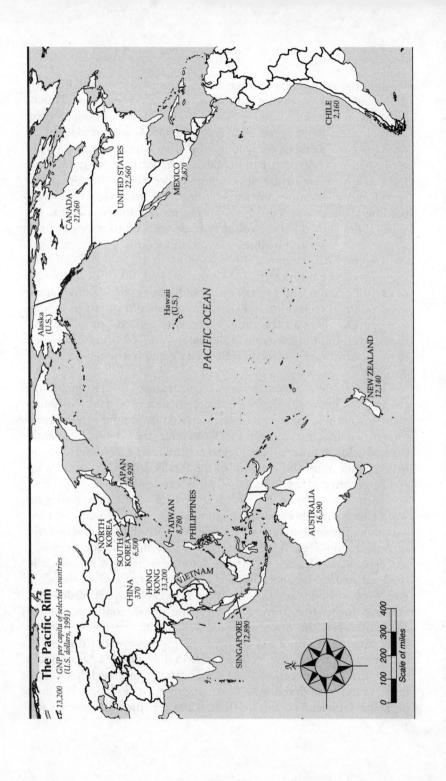

The Pacific Rim

₵ 13,200 · GNP per capita of selected countries
(U.S. dollars, 1991)

CANADA
21,260

UNITED STATES
22,560

Alaska
(U.S.)

MEXICO
2,870

CHILE
2,160

Hawaii
(U.S.)

PACIFIC OCEAN

NEW ZEALAND
12,140

JAPAN
26,920

NORTH
KOREA

SOUTH
KOREA
6,500

TAIWAN
8,780

PHILIPPINES

CHINA
370

HONG
KONG
13,200

VIETNAM

AUSTRALIA
16,590

SINGAPORE
12,890

0   100   200   300   400

Scale of miles

lessly made or lackadaisically marketed and that American workers were unmotivated and unproductive.

Top officials of the two countries attempted to moderate the tone of communications across the Pacific, but less responsible types on both sides played to audiences often inclined to think the worst of those strange people beyond the ocean. The American trade deficit with Japan sparked repeated calls from lobbyists and legislators for protection of American producers against Japanese imports and for stern measures to pry Japanese markets open to American exports. Through the end of 1994, the Bush and Clinton administrations resisted most of the protectionist demands; free trade remained the goal if not the unexceptioned practice.

Economics also lay at the heart of American relations with the other countries of the Western Hemisphere. After doing its best for most of a century to build a wall between the U.S. economy and its own, the Mexican government, now under President Carlos Salinas (an economist by education), opted for just the reverse: a free-trade agreement between Mexico and the United States. The agreement would be joined to a preexisting pact between the United States and Canada, with the resulting North American Free Trade Agreement producing a free-trade zone from the Yucatan to the Arctic. Proponents of NAFTA held that it would stimulate the economies of the three countries, providing greater prosperity for all. As an added attraction for the United States, it would diminish the incentive of Mexicans to immigrate (often illegally) to the United States, since it would boost Mexican incomes. Opponents of NAFTA predicted a flight of American jobs across the Rio Grande to low-wage Mexico; NAFTA foe and 1992 presidential candidate H. Ross Perot said Americans would hear "a giant sucking sound" as employment went south. The Bush administration strongly supported NAFTA before handing the still-unapproved (by Congress) agreement to the Clinton administration, which also supported it, but not quite as wholeheartedly. Yet at the eleventh hour Clinton threw his full weight behind the pact, and in the decisive vote in the House of Representatives the free-traders carried the day. The Senate seconded the result shortly afterward, and on January 1, 1994, the first stage of the agreement took effect.[11]

The Clinton administration struck another blow for free trade at

---

[11]Ross Perot, *Not for Sale at Any Price* (New York, 1993), 133.

the end of 1994 when it persuaded Congress to approve the latest version of the General Agreement on Tariffs and Trade. The GATT accord, which embraced more than one hundred nations, would cut tariffs substantially over several years. Protectionists delayed U.S. ratification; then congressional Republicans, full of themselves following smashing G.O.P. victories in the November 1994 elections, taunted Clinton and the Democrats and threatened to cause trouble. But the deal turned out to be too promising to pass up. After the requisite posturing, both houses approved by comfortable margins.

A regional version of free trade continued to make progress in Europe, under the auspices of the European Union, the group of twelve Western European nations that in 1992 had eliminated almost all barriers to the free flow of trade, labor, and investment among member states. The European Union had grown out of the earlier European (Economic) Community, also called the Common Market, and in doing so had acquired certain practices and institutions that weren't simply economic, including a European parliament and associated bureaucracies. Ambitious Euro-unifiers desired to go still further, toward something like a United States of Europe. A recession during the early 1990s, along with the confusion consequent to the end of the Cold War, the reunification of Germany, and the breakup of the Soviet empire, threw unexpected hurdles in the way of this more comprehensive unification. But even if the E.U. continued to be chiefly an economic entity, it promised to be something Americans would have to pay close attention to. The E.U. comprised the largest market in the world (in terms of value of trade), with all the potential for good or ill such a distinction implied. If the Europeans opened their doors to American imports, American exporters might see a surge in sales. If the Europeans closed their doors, creating what pessimists called a "Fortress Europe," American exporters might suffer seriously. That the decision in the matter was up to the Europeans demonstrated yet again how direction of the world economy had slipped away from the United States.

For what it was worth, Americans could take some solace from the fact that the relative decline they were experiencing appeared to be inherent in the evolution of mature economies. Newly industrializing countries generally grow faster than fully industrialized countries, not least because the productivity gains resulting from the initial application of machines to manufacturing processes are greater than those resulting from subsequent refinements of industrial techniques. Oversimplified: the percentage difference in output per hour between a woman sewing shirts by hand and one using a sewing machine is greater than the difference between a woman using a sewing machine and one using a better sewing machine. During the 1980s and early 1990s, the fastest-growing economies belonged not to Japan and Germany, the stars of an earlier generation, but to China and the so-called four dragons (sometimes "tigers") of East Asia: Taiwan, Singapore, Hong Kong, and South Korea. Just as American prosperity had tended to price American workers out of certain unskilled jobs during the 1950s and 1960s, so prosperity in Japan and Germany tended to price Japanese and German workers out of unskilled jobs during the 1980s and 1990s. Many of those jobs went to China and the other newly industrializing countries, where labor costs were lower. This development didn't restore many jobs to the United States (although by the early 1990s labor costs in America had fallen below those of Japan and Germany), but it made Americans feel they weren't alone in facing a future of slower growth.

A future of slower growth appeared to be one of the few things Americans could count on in the second half of the 1990s. The heady days of unquestioned prosperity, when each generation took for granted that it would live better than its parents, had evidently passed. The United States was hardly the economic weakling doom-sayers sometimes made it out to be, and the American gross domestic product remained by far the largest of any single country in the world. But where in the late 1940s American industrial production had almost matched that of the rest of humanity combined, by the mid-1990s the United States was merely first among equals—and not always first—in matters of economics.

Other aspects of the future appeared less definite. Eastern Europe and parts of the former Soviet Union were in turmoil. In some countries the turmoil was mostly political and economic, but in several former Soviet republics, not to mention in the former Yugoslavia, armed conflict was commonplace. That four of the successor states to the Soviet Union possessed nuclear weapons didn't contribute to the sound sleep of people disposed to worry. The three smaller nuclear heirs—Ukraine, Belarus, and Kazakhstan—ultimately agreed to give up their nuclear arms (in exchange for promises of Western aid); this allowed the implementation of the Strategic Arms Reduction Treaty (START), which had been signed by Washington and Moscow in 1991 but delayed by the disintegration of the Soviet Union. When fully in effect, START would significantly diminish the number of nuclear warheads in the world. But the worrywarts still fretted about the thousands of big bombs that remained, as well as about the possibility that terrorists or other undesirables might get their hands on some of the supposedly deactivated nuclear devices.

The Middle East was hardly more reassuring. Saddam Hussein retained power in Iraq, somewhat less aggressive than before the Persian Gulf War of 1991 but hardly less fractious. The Islamic republic of Iran regularly announced its intention to bring the rest of the Middle East to the teachings of the Prophet Muhammad as interpreted by the Iranian mullahs; Iran's leaders didn't rule out force as a tool of redemption. Elsewhere in the Middle East, other Islamic militants grew more active by the day. The government of Egypt, the most populous of the Arab states, found itself under constant attack from the religious radicals. Although the Arab-Israeli dispute hadn't provoked a regular war for over ten years, the Palestinians in the occupied territories had engaged in an *intifada* (uprising) against the Israeli occupiers for half a decade. A historic 1993 agreement between the Israeli government and the Palestine Liberation Organization, facilitated politically and economically by the Clinton administration, and signed at the White House, produced the first steps toward Palestinian self-government and perhaps a Palestinian state (and made a 1994 Israel-Jordan peace treaty possible), but the agreement elicited bitter and sometimes violent opposition among both Israelis and Palestinians, and its future appeared problematic.

Central America was quieter than in years but hardly silent. The Sandinistas in Nicaragua had responded to the end of the contra war by holding long-promised elections, which, to their surprise, they lost. The conservatives who replaced them (only some of them: in the interest of national unity the government of Violeta Chamorro left some Sandinistas in their old posts) promised a new day in Nicaraguan affairs. But they delivered only a new few hours. Many of the same problems that had provoked the Sandinista revolution in the first place resurfaced, and some of the Sandinista veterans once more took to the hills. The contras responded by reshouldering arms themselves. At one point during the summer of 1993, a squad of Sandinistas held one group of hostages in one part of the country while contra commandos held another group in another part. Though Washington had greeted the arrival of Chamorro with enthusiasm, by the mid-1990s almost no Americans wanted to get deeply reinvolved in Nicaraguan affairs. The Clinton administration found it easy to ignore the country that had obsessed the Reagan administration a decade earlier.

The Democratic administration found Haiti harder to ignore. That Caribbean nation had long been desperately poor, to the extent that tens of thousands of Haitians chanced the hazardous sea passage to the United States to escape their plight. Their burdens were increased in 1991 when a band of military officers deposed the elected president, Jean-Bertrand Aristide, and waged a campaign of intimidation against his backers. The United States government, in the interests of hemispheric democracy and diminished Haitian emigration, attempted diplomatically to arrange Aristide's return to power. Washington also enforced United Nations-approved economic sanctions against Haiti and its rulers. When the diplomatic efforts and the economic sanctions proved unavailing, the Clinton administration escalated to military measures—almost. In September 1994, Clinton threatened an invasion of Haiti; indeed, he gave the order for the first airborne squadrons to lift off from the United States and head south. At the last minute, though, Haiti's junta saw reason and agreed to leave peacefully. The American invasion became an essentially uncontested intervention and then a comparatively quiet occupation. Aristide arrived in mid-October. More than 20,000 U.S. troops helped him establish his authority.

The Clinton administration adopted a lower profile in other areas, including some, like Central America, where its predecessors had invested many American resources and much American prestige. The Afghan civil war continued, but without American involvement. (Despite the role American assistance to the mujahideen had played in persuading the Soviets to leave Afghanistan, some American officials began to regret that assistance when leftover American weapons started showing up on the international black market and in the arsenals of terrorists.) Peace had broken out in Cambodia, but how long it would last depended on the willingness of the Khmer Rouge cadres to accept the leadership of factions and individuals they had done their best to exterminate. Washington left it to other governments to oversee Cambodia's attempted transition to normal life after a quarter century of civil war, genocide, self-inflicted famine, and lesser calamities.

The Angolan civil war sputtered on, but at a lower level of violence than before. Occasionally peace threatened to disrupt the fighting. In part the reduced violence was the result of the end of the Cold War and the superpower subsidies the Soviet-American competition had brought, but it was also a consequence of the landmark development of the 1990s in the region: the transition of South Africa from white-dominated apartheid to multiracial democracy. The United States could claim a minor amount of credit for the transition; along with most other countries it had imposed economic sanctions against the old regime. But most of the credit was due to Nelson Mandela and the myriad others in South Africa itself who had fought and suffered (in Mandela's case, spending a quarter century in prison) for racial and political equality.

The news from farther north in Africa was considerably worse. Chronic tension in Rwanda gave way in the spring of 1994 to massacres that mounted to genocide. The Clinton administration condemned the violence and lamented the tragedy but, pointing out that no vital American interests were at stake, and noting that American public support for intervention was not even half-hearted—more like quarter- or eighth-hearted—took no substantive measures to stop the killing.

Amid the rapid changes around the globe, there were few obvious guideposts for American foreign policy. "Nations need enemies," wrote conservative commentator Charles Krauthammer as the Cold War was winding down; for forty years after World War II the most dangerous enemy had been obvious to most Americans. And the identity of the enemy had strongly shaped American policy. Different persons and parties might differ regarding the best method of dealing with the Soviet Union, but none disputed that the Soviet Union needed to be dealt with. Richard Nixon and Henry Kissinger had pursued detente in the early 1970s, contending that engagement rather than constant confrontation was the most fruitful method of handling Moscow. Jimmy Carter went further in the same direction, proposing American moral principles as the best defense against Soviet cynicism and the most promising route to true American security. The pendulum swung back in Carter's final year, and swung farther under Ronald Reagan, to renewed confrontation and a revived Cold War. But then the rise of Mikhail Gorbachev pushed the pendulum once more in the direction of engagement and coexistence.[12]

With the collapse of the Soviet Union, the cable holding the pendulum broke. Whether American leaders roasted the Soviets or toasted them, the mere existence of the Soviet Union as the other superpower had conferred a satisfying symmetry and a reassuring simplicity on American dealings with the world. The crackup of the Soviet Union destroyed the symmetry and revealed the world in all its appalling complexity. Since Vietnam, Americans had tried by one means or other to deny this complexity. Denial was now no longer an option.

Yet there was a positive side to the situation. Many of the failures of recent American policy had resulted from this vain search for simplicity. If events of late precluded a further search, that might be all to the good. Better the real than the merely reassuring.

[12]H. W. Brands, *The Devil We Knew* (New York, 1993), 206.

Sources and Suggestions

The footnotes to the foregoing chapters cite only the sources of direct quotations. In many cases these sources include the most valuable works on their respective subjects, but not always. The following essay is intended to fill out this source base and, even more importantly, to suggest to students where they might find additional information on subjects that strike their fancy.

A good place to begin any investigation of diplomacy is with the diplomats. Richard Nixon and Henry Kissinger have to come first, given the time frame of this book. Nixon has been the subject of dozens of studies and was the author of almost as many books of his own. His memoirs (*RN: The Memoirs of Richard Nixon*, 1978) are defensive—if you had done what he did, your memoirs would be too. But they are quite detailed and illuminate his thinking. His subsequent books, culminating in the posthumous *Beyond Peace* (1994), plow much of the same ground, in geopolitical philosophy if not in explicit subject matter.

Of the Nixon biographies, the most thorough is Stephen Ambrose's balanced three-volume *Nixon* (1987–91). This is also the best biography for foreign affairs, reflecting Ambrose's background as a diplomatic historian. Garry Wills, in *Nixon Agonistes* (1970), captures an aspect of the personality, though he writes too early to say much about the president as president or about his foreign policy. Herbert Parmet (*Richard Nixon and His America*, 1990) and Tom Wicker (*One of Us*, 1991) place Nixon in contemporary context. Jonathan Aitken (*Nixon*, 1993) is very sympathetic. Not a Nixon biography but the most revealing inside view of the thirty-seventh president in office is H. R. Haldeman's posthumous *The Haldeman Diaries* (1994).

The place to begin on Kissinger is his double-barreled memoir (*White House Years*, 1979; *Years of Upheaval*, 1982). These books are enormously detailed and are almost entirely concerned with foreign affairs. They can be slow going: as one reviewer remarked of Kissinger, after having survived the two volumes, the author might not be a great writer, but anyone who gets to the end is a great reader. Like Nixon, Kissinger continued to explain and reinterpret his actions; his *Diplomacy* (1994) is a monumental study that provides historical and theoretical justification for his actions as national security adviser and secretary of state.

Of the Kissinger biographies, Walter Isaacson's *Kissinger* (1992) is the most judicious and comprehensive. Robert Schulzinger's *Henry Kissinger* (1989) is stronger on Kissinger's diplomacy per se—Schulzinger being another diplomatic historian. Seymour Hersh's *The Price of Power* (1983) is unrelentingly, but not undeservedly, critical.

Gerald Ford's cameo role in American foreign policy is covered unexceptionally in his *A Time to Heal* (1978).

Members of the Carter administration continued in their memoirs the battles they started while in office. Carter's own *Keeping Faith* (1982) is earnest and intelligent, as one would expect. Cyrus Vance's *Hard Choices* (1983) is a lawyer's brief for the positions adopted by the secretary of state. Zbigniew Brzezinski's *Power and Principle* (1983) is the most fun of the three; the only places he buries hatchets are in the necks of his rivals.

Outsiders viewing the Carter administration have had difficulty applauding the Democratic president's achievements. Gaddis Smith's *Morality, Reason, and Power* (1986) credits Carter's intentions but finds his implementation often lacking. Richard Thornton (*The Carter Years*, 1991) and Donald Spencer (*The Carter Implosion*, 1988) can only shake their heads at Carter's amateurishness.

Though the American people loved Ronald Reagan, it's hard to tell why from the literature on the Republican president. This isn't entirely because most academics and journalists are anti-Reagan liberals. Reagan's own *An American Life* (1990) reads like many of the president's famous anecdotes—but over hundreds of pages it gets tiring. Alexander Haig has little nice to say in *Caveat* (1984), which essentially explains how everyone in the administration was out to get him. Donald Regan likewise lays waste to many of his colleagues in *For the Record* (1988). David Stockman, in *The Triumph of Politics* (1986), sees cynicism behind the sunny facade. More favorable to the president, if not to their administration mates, are George Shultz in *Turmoil and Triumph* (1993) and Caspar Weinberger in *Fighting for Peace* (1990). Robert McFarlane gives the view from the national security adviser's office in *Special Trust* (1994); Constantine Menges provides a similar view from a lower angle in *Inside the National Security Council* (1988).

Reagan still resides in the realm of journalism rather than history, since most of the important documents dealing with his two terms remain classified and beyond reach. Of the journalists, none knew Reagan better than Lou Cannon, whose *President Reagan* (1991) is one of the best works of its kind in recent memory. Haynes Johnson offers another journalistic perspective in *Sleepwalking through History* (1991). Diplomatic historian Michael Schaller tries his hand at contemporary history (if such a thing exists) in *Reckoning with Reagan* (1992).

Once past the personalities, the student can tackle the literature on specific subjects. Nearly all aspects of American foreign policy during the last twenty-five years have provoked controversy; that controversy shows clearly in the literature.

Retired diplomat and continuing Soviet specialist Raymond Garthoff has written the mother of all detente sourcebooks: *Detente and Confrontation* (1985). Garthoff's magnum opus is more than almost anyone would want to read about detente, at least all at once, but it is a fountain of information and a demonstration of what can be done with the public record by someone with insight and industry.

Garthoff, who has been associated with the mildly liberal Brookings Institution, looks relatively favorably on detente; at the opposite end of the spectrum is Norman Podhoretz's *The Present Danger* (1980). Podhoretz is as short on facts as Garthoff is long, and as long on vitriol as Garthoff is short. But the book, which came out just in time for the 1980 election, is a must read for anyone who wants to understand the passions detente aroused.

Better informed than Podhoretz's book but less detailed than Garthoff's are Adam Ulam's *Dangerous Relations* (1983), a skeptical interpretation of detente focusing on Moscow's actions and intentions; Richard Pipes's *U.S.-Soviet Relations in the Era of Detente* (1981), more skeptical; and William Hyland's *Mortal Rivals* (1987), less skeptical (which is not surprising, in that Hyland worked to promote detente under Nixon, Ford, and Carter).

On the subfield of detente relating to arms control, Charles Morris (*Iron Destinies, Lost Opportunities*, 1988) and Ronald Powaski (*March to Armageddon*, 1987) offer perspective. Strobe Talbott's *Endgame* (1979) zeroes in on SALT II. Talbott's *Deadly Gambits* (1984) carries the story into the Reagan years, while his *The Master of the Game* (1988) traces the activities of one negotiator (Paul Nitze).

Issues touching the Middle East have been fully as controversial as Soviet-American relations. But start with a balanced—naturally—survey: H. W. Brands's *Into the Labyrinth* (1994). Then try a more opinionated rendering, on the specific subject of U.S. relations with Israel and the Arab states: Stephen Spiegel's *The Other Arab-Israeli Conflict* (1985). Escalate again to George Ball and Douglas Ball's *The Passionate Attachment* (1993), which castigates U.S. policy as heedlessly pro-Israel; Yossi Melman and Dan Raviv's *Friends in Deed* (1994), which praises Washington for what the Balls blast it for; and Avi Shlaim's *War and Peace in the Middle East* (1994), which largely agrees with the Balls but for somewhat different reasons. By way of a return to reasoned and dispassionate analysis, consult two by William Quandt: *Decade of Decisions* (1977), on the prelude and postlude to the 1973 war; and *Camp David* (1986).

As turbulent as Israel's immediate neighborhood has been Iran. Almost no study devoted to Iran specifically has anything good to say about American policy during the 1970s and 1980s. This is a fair enough judgment, given Washington's role in the shah's downfall, the hostage crisis, and the Iran-contra affair. (The only important defenses of American actions are in the memoirs of the policymakers themselves, cited above.) Three solid works are Barry Rubin's *Paved with Good Intentions* (1980), critical of everyone from Eisenhower to Carter; James Bill's *The Eagle and the Lion* (1988), more critical still, and by someone who warned the Carter administration of the cataclysm to come; and Gary Sick's *All Fall Down* (1985), an insider's lament.

Libya, that other bête noire of American presidents, hasn't generated much accessible literature. But two books are useful: Edward Haley's *Qaddafi and the United States since 1969* (1984) and Brian

Davis's *Qaddafi, Terrorism, and the Origins of the U.S. Attack on Libya* (1990).

The Persian Gulf War of 1991 is too recent for sound historical treatment. First place in a weak field goes to Lawrence Freedman and Efraim Karsh's *The Gulf Conflict 1990–1991* (1992). Bob Woodward digs into the struggle that took place behind the scenes in Washington in *The Commanders* (1991). Roger Hilsman characterizes the conflict in *mano a mano* terms in *George Bush vs. Saddam Hussein* (1992). Rick Atkinson tells the obligatory "untold story" in *Crusade* (1993).

Certain recent events benefit (the public, not the perpetrators) from being so controversial as to provoke congressional investigations. In such cases documents get subpoenaed and declassified and suspects and witnesses get sworn to tell the truth (although not all do, as Oliver North demonstrated). The Iran-contra affair—speaking of North—falls into this category. By far the most thorough and readable account is Theodore Draper's *A Very Thin Line* (1991). The official *Report of the Congressional Committees Investigating the Iran-Contra Affair* (1987) and numerous supporting volumes are packed with intriguing minutiae. William S. Cohen and George J. Mitchell (*Men of Zeal*, 1988) explain what the Iran-contra hearings sounded like to the legislative investigators. Gary Sick suggests that the shady business with Iran ran deeper, at least back to the 1980 election (*October Surprise*, 1991). Bob Woodward, in *Veil* (1987), transcribes William Casey's mumbles. Joseph Persico, in *Casey* (1990), covers the career.

At the opposite end of the Iran-contra pipeline from the Middle East was Central America. The ever provocative Walter LaFeber, in the best overview of U.S.-Central American relations (*Inevitable Revolutions*, 1992), asserts that the troubles of the region owed much to American meddling, which, while aiming for stability, created the very conditions that made stability impossible. In other words, Carter's troubles in Nicaragua were nothing new. Robert Pastor (*Condemned to Repetition*, 1987) and Anthony Lake (*Somoza Falling*, 1989) explain the dilemmas facing the United States as they appeared from Washington. Roy Gutman (*Banana Diplomacy*, 1988) covers the contra war as critically, in his own way, as LaFeber. Thomas Carothers (*In the Name of Democracy*, 1991) is more academic and less confrontational. Other titles worth a look are Mary Vanderlaan's *Revolution and Foreign Policy in Nicaragua* (1986) and E. Bradford Burns's *At War in Nicaragua* (1987). On the separate but related topic of Panama and the 1989 American invasion, journalist Kevin Buckley is critical and well-informed (*Panama*, 1991).

The end of the Cold War has spawned almost as much debate as its beginning. The two best accounts, factually, are Don Oberdorfer's *The Turn* (1991), which covers the period from the downing of the Korean airliner in 1983 almost to the reunification of Germany in 1990; and Michael Beschloss and Strobe Talbott's *At the Highest Levels* (1993), a fly-on-the-wall treatment of the shorter period from the beginning of the Bush administration to the dissolution of the Soviet Union. A vivid rendering of the Soviet breakup is David Remnick's *Lenin's Tomb* (1993). Interpretations of the end of the Cold War range from the pro-Reagan, celebratory *Victory*, by Peter Schweizer (1994), to the rain-on-your-parade *We All Lost the Cold War*, by Richard Lebow and Janice Stein (1994). H. W. Brands, in *The Devil We Knew* (1993), wonders what Americans will do now that their trusty old enemy has vanished. Joseph Nye says they'd better do what they've been doing all along, in *Bound to Lead* (1990).

Lebow and Stein, Brands, and Nye assess economic issues such as the American trade and budget deficits; Paul Kennedy makes economics the centerpiece of his best-selling *The Rise and Fall of the Great Powers* (1987). Kennedy suggests that America's reach may by now have exceeded its grasp. David Calleo, in *The Imperious Economy* (1982), examines similar questions more narrowly, as do Robert Solomon in *The International Monetary System* (1977) and Joanne Gowa in *Closing the Gold Window* (1983). These last two authors carefully cover the breakdown of the Bretton Woods system.

The emergence of Japan as an economic superpower has started Americans asking whether they ought to be worried, and whether they ought to emulate Japan. Both Clyde Prestowitz (*Trading Places*, 1988) and James Fallows (*Looking at the Sun*, 1994) counsel a combination of worry and emulation; Bill Emmott (*The Sun Also Sets*, 1989) tells Americans and other non-Japanese to take it easy.

Most matters of international economics are dull; the major exception is oil. Daniel Yergin tells a rollicking tale, but also delivers an astute analysis, in *The Prize* (1991); nonfiction doesn't come much better than this. Anthony Sampson is more rollicking but less astute in *The Seven Sisters* (1988). For those who think economics and business *ought* to be dull, there are always Steven Schneider's *The Oil Price Revolution* (1983) and Dankwart Rustow's *Oil and Turmoil* (1982), both of which focus on the 1970s.

Index

Index

DATE DUE